Brenda Krause Eheart is one of the great social innovators of our time—and *Neighbors* brings together all she has learned over many years toiling at the intersection of people, proximity, and the potential for genuine human connection. It is an eloquent blueprint for how we can rediscover our relationships, find enduring happiness, and create communities where everyone thrives.

—Marc Freedman
Founder/CEO of Encore.org
Author of *How to Live Forever*

Neighbors comes at a critical time in our global experience. At a time when physical and political separation has emerged at a scale we have never experienced, a solution is within our grasp that draws on the power of ordinary people to do extraordinary things.

—Niranjan S. Karnik, MD, PhD
Associate Dean for Community Behavioral Health
Rush University

When Brenda Eheart saw how children in foster care were all too often rejected by one family after the next, she set out to do something about it. She persuaded the Pentagon to give her 80 houses on an Air Force Base scheduled for closure. She populated this new neighborhood with families willing to adopt these kids and then added older and retired adults who in no time became surrogate grandparents. *Neighbors* is the story of community built to heal children but which ended up healing seniors as well.

This book is inspiring, written with verve, heart and love. I couldn't stop reading.

—Lesley Stahl
Correspondent, CBS *Sixty Minutes*
Author of *Becoming Grandma*

Eheart's book is fresh air—oxygen for a dysfunctional culture. In a time when support systems are breaking down and threads of connection are fraying, *Neighbors* offers hope. Not just through feel-good aspiration, but with a credible vision anchored in compelling stories, research, and real-life examples.

We can design buildings and shared spaces to support personal wellbeing and social connection, and we can call on government and social services to solve intractable problems. These are all good and essential, but they can't replace what Eheart shows as the missing ingredient in our lives and in our communities—caring relationships.

I look forward to letting others know about *Neighbors*! It offers a potent vision for change as we emerge from this global pandemic.

—Ross Chapin, FAIA
Ross Chapin Architects
Author of *Pocket Neighborhoods: Creating Small Scale Community in a Large Scale World*

In our increasingly disconnected world, *Neighbors* proposes a path forward: a new way to address obstacles to wellbeing engaging an entirely new category of experts, the people next door. Not just any neighbors, however, but neighbors of all ages. Brenda Eheart's intentional, intergenerational communities unleash the power that can only be found when we truly respect and engage people of all ages and abilities. Now more than ever, the capacity neighbors have to heal and unite us may be our nation's most valuable social commodity.

—Donna Butts
Executive Director
Generations United

Neighbors

BRENDA KRAUSE EHEART

Neighbors

THE POWER OF THE PEOPLE NEXT DOOR

Belong Press
Champaign, Illinois

NEIGHBORS: The Power of the People Next Door

Published by Belong Press
Champaign, Illinois
www.buildingohana.org/neighbors-power-of-people-next-door

First Print Edition

ISBN 978-1-7351759-0-4 (softcover)
ISBN 978-1-7351759-1-1 (ebook)

Cover design: Yvonne Parks, PearCreative.ca
Interior design and typeset: Katherine Lloyd, The DESK
Back cover author photo credit: Jim Harrison

To my family—Wayland, Sarah, and Seth,

To my friend and colleague—Carolyn Casteel,

and

To the founding residents of Hope Meadows

Human relationships are primary in all of living. When the gusty winds blow and shake our lives, if we know that people care about us, we may bend with the wind...but we won't break.[1]

—Fred Rogers,
The World According to Mister Rogers

Contents

Foreword

As I began to write the "foreword" to this book, I started to think about its closely related homophone, the word "forward," defined as that which is "in the front or toward the future." I even looked the word up, half-expecting the definition to include a photo of my good friend, Brenda Eheart. She was, after all, there at the beginning of this modern exploration of intergenerational reciprocity and she has always been oriented toward the future. In *Neighbors* she does not disappoint, helping us once again envision a path forward.

Neighbors describes Eheart's journey, a journey of love and understanding and of insights painfully won that must be vigorously protected. It is also "our journey," as she has shared this path so wisely and generously with so many. There is nothing in the pages that follow to suggest that this journey was easy and like most good things on this green earth, the way forward is difficult. Fortunately, difficult journeys have the power to summon patience and persistence from reservoirs that in the end we know were there all along.

Mary Pipher's book *The Shelter of Each Other* addresses the myriad ways we have come to build, reinforce, and, in some ways become prisoners of, a culture that is distinctly unfriendly to families. It includes a bit of advice which I think is native to Eheart's work: to "protect from what is harmful and connect to what is beautiful." This is the essence of Hope Meadows and the human alchemy that results when people of different ages, abilities, needs, dreams, experiences, and backgrounds are encouraged to form vibrant and enduring communities of mutual concern.

Neighbors is heartfelt and jargon free. It is offered as a soulful guide to making soulful communities and deserves to be studied as such. You can hear Brenda Eheart's voice as you turn its pages. She is speaking to us, telling us the secrets that it took her a lifetime to unlock and inviting us to transform her work into new forms that serve people in new ways and in new places. This is a challenge we would be wise to accept, never doubting that the Hope Meadows story, really the ancient and ever renewed story of "good neighboring," can help us all find a path forward—together.

—Dr. Bill Thomas, Geriatrician
Author, and founder of Eden Alternative,
The Green House Project, and ChangingAging.org

Introduction

> Hope is not the same as joy that things are going well, or willingness to invest in enterprises that are obviously headed for early success, but rather an ability to work for something because it is good.[1]
>
> —Václav Havel, *Disturbing the Peace*

PIONEERS

Elmer and Margie Davis risked everything to move to Hope Meadows. We first met there in January 1995—in the middle of a blizzard. They'd just driven over 1000 miles from their retirement home in Florida, having pulled up all roots to move, sight unseen, to this five-block, nontraditional neighborhood in Illinois, where senior residents would offer caring support to adoptive families and their children.

Why, I wondered, would a retired couple in their seventies want to leave Florida's warm weather, sandy beaches, and ocean sunsets for the corn and soybean fields of landlocked Central Illinois, a place where older people often feel trapped by the weather in their homes from November to April? Florida is America's retirement haven—the place to go to find happiness, enjoyment, and leisure in our later years. Illinois is not.

I knew little about Elmer except that over the years he had held various blue-collar jobs and finally retired as a machinist. Recently recovered from triple by-pass surgery, he lived on a modest, fixed income with his wife of half a century. Margie was a small woman, and quiet, but her eyes sparkled with humor and wisdom. From their son, who read about us in the news, they learned of Hope—an intergenerational, intentional neighborhood located a little more than two hours south of Chicago. He thought it might be just the place for his parents, and especially for his dad, whose golden years weren't going so well.

Still, I was worried. It seemed to me that life at Hope Meadows would be the polar opposite of the "good life" in Florida. Yet on that day in January, there stood seventy-six-year-old Elmer, dressed for the freezing cold in his new winter cap, jacket, and gloves, grinning ear-to-ear. He was, from all appearances, happy to be home and ready to get to work.

As we walked from the driveway to the front door of their new home, three neighborhood kids ran up with shovels to clear the way. Others unloaded the car, which was packed to the gills. Neighbors appeared like apparitions through the blowing snow, closing in from all directions to greet and welcome their new Hope friends.

Weeks later Margie confided, "Elmer was bored in Florida. He wouldn't get up and walk; he wouldn't do anything—just watched television from morning to night." And, she added, "Down there, nobody neighbored." Living in Hope Meadows, she believed, would change things; her husband's new role in the community would give him a reason to live again. Elmer needed to feel needed, to know that people cared and that his life had purpose and meaning in spite of his age and health problems. Like so many others of his generation, a fundamental need to be meaningfully connected to others was not being met. Upon his retirement in Florida, those connections had been severed.

A year after Elmer and Margie moved in, an *ABC News Nightline* crew visited Hope Meadows to do a story on what was still a new and unfolding neighborhood like no other. When they interviewed Elmer, he explained how his life had changed: "I've had open-heart surgery; I've got a pacemaker, and I'm a diabetic to boot—and [now] I'm having a good time!"[2] And when they asked me—its founder—how I'd first envisioned Hope Meadows, I admitted I'd never thought of it as a real neighborhood at all, much less one so closely connected and so diversely composed of families and individuals of all ages and life experiences. The *Nightline* crew continued their visits over several months and produced hours of film interviewing residents and showing daily life in the community. Ted Koppel—expecting to host the standard ten-minute *Nightline* segment—reviewed it all and decided the Hope story deserved a full half-hour on national TV. Hope Meadows turned out to surprise us all.

National media often refer to Hope Meadows as an intentional retirement community. It didn't start out that way, nor is this all that it is. Hope was originally designed to be an alternative to the revolving door of foster care, a place where neglected and abused children—specifically those who desperately needed adoptive parents—would find them. It would be a place where twelve to fifteen single parents and couples would live next to and support one another as they worked to successfully raise the children who came to them with highly troubled pasts. It wasn't until we installed mailboxes in front of every home, and I first saw the USPS truck crawling through our streets and stopping at every residence that I realized the truth: Hope was indeed an honest-to-goodness American neighborhood!

Hope Meadows quickly evolved into an intergenerational community with not only a dozen or so homes for children and their foster-adoptive parents, but also with spacious apartments for many *grandfriends* like Elmer and Margie.[3] It grew into a neighborhood of people from all walks of life, a place where nearly all its residents became integral to the health, safety, and happiness of one another. Hope came to represent a kind of community-based humanity where older adults made an intentional commitment to be family, friends, and thoughtful neighbors—to care in times of trouble or illness, to comfort in loss, to celebrate in joy, to teach, to share, to help, to protect, and so much more. The relationships that emerged from these commitments formed the foundation of daily life at Hope, reliable havens of healing and belonging that deepened regardless of age, vulnerability, education, position, or experience. Hope residents transformed not only the lives of those most vulnerable, but their own lives as well, providing a template of community life for others to follow. Here the ordinary became the extraordinary, bringing people together when all around us, it seemed, we were growing farther and farther apart.

"SEEM[S] REAL, BUT MOST OF US DON'T LIVE THERE."

For decades it's been the hope of contemporary culture that technology will be the force that heals and unites us. But management and software design experts Tom DeMarco and Timothy Lister know differently, contending that most of the problems within their own industry are human, or "sociological" rather than technological, and that tech company leaders ignore these problems at their peril.[4] As early as 1987, they tellingly named modern culture and community as contributing factors: "Western heritage, particularly American heritage, is rich in the lore of Community. Our literature and films are full of the image of the American small town where you stroll past the picket fences of your neighbors, waving hello and stopping to chat with the butcher or to pet the druggist's collie." The features of this small town or neighborhood vision, they go on to say, "seem real, but most of us don't live there. Instead we live in a modern noncommunity."[5] It is perhaps the stark contrast of these two views that prompted Ted Koppel to introduce Hope Meadows as a neighborhood "so old-fashioned it's, well...new."[6]

Today, the modern *noncommunity* thrives, encouraged by the use of social media, and leaving us further isolated from face-to-face contact, intimate verbal conversation, and even genuinely warm physical touch. All are essential for the development of caring relationships and to our overall wellbeing. It seems clear that little by little, our collective ability to care for the welfare of others is diminished as our individual efforts become less direct, less personal, and even somewhat superficial. It is one kind of engagement, for example, to text back and forth with a friend who has lost a loved one. It is another experience entirely when you are physically present for that friend, listening to her, comforting her with a hug, and offering a tissue to wipe her tears away. If you don't believe it, imagine which of these two encounters you would remember with gratitude years down the road.

Further, in our modern noncommunity, a ubiquitous social media network has left us shell-shocked as headlines, posts, and tweets remind us of the growing differences between us. Carved from opposing beliefs, backgrounds and experiences, they encourage our tendency to divide into fearful and highly opinionated tribes where civility often seems to be nonexistent.

When we become more disconnected and divided, our inability to come together to address the challenging social problems in front of us actually becomes part of the problem. The challenges are clear: The opioid epidemic is ripping families apart, and all around us are the consequences of poverty, racism, violence, corruption, child and elder abuse, the housing crisis, unaffordable health care, an influx of refugees, the utter loneliness of aging, and a lack of compassionate and quality end of life care. The list is longer than even this, resulting in a social crisis about which we are better informed, more polarized and angrier than ever. When added to the weight of our own complicated lives, these enormous problems—some very close to home—can seem too much to bear.

How will so many problems be solved and by whom? When I am most discouraged, I ask myself, "Can they be solved?" and I wonder, "What can everyday people—really all of us in our everyday lives—possibly do to make a difference?" Courtney Martin, author and blogger, tellingly writes, "We read the news, then retreat from it, unsure how to process the problems that abound, or be part of potential solutions to those problems."[7]

Meanwhile solutions—at least partial ones—do emerge: expanding tax credits for the poor, more funding for community colleges, and investment in affordable housing to name a few. These approaches, although limited in scope, make sense and can be effective. But, because they are often created within the seemingly impenetrable walls of "systems" and "institutions," they are also complicated and expensive, highly regulated and thus often inflexible, and most certainly beyond the purview of everyday people who want to make a significant contribution.

We ask ourselves, "What can I possibly do to provide tax relief or more affordable housing? What can I do to address the problems associated with the institutionalization of kids in foster care, of people with intellectual and developmental disabilities, or of our oldest citizens?" And the truthful answer is "Not much." We can vote, to be sure, and we can volunteer our time and money to worthy causes. We can work in a soup kitchen, or donate clothes, but having a hand in transformative systems change is typically out of our reach. We feel disqualified, and this often leads to our "retreat" and sometimes to giving up all together as a kind of hopelessness ensues and we ask, "Why bother?"

When I feel this kind of powerlessness, I think of the people of Hope Meadows, people like Elmer and Margie, and they give me great hope. They taught me that *ordinary people of all ages and experiences, through their everyday acts of care and kindness, with guidance and a shared purpose, can create a culture of neighborliness and caring, empowering all of us to become, not bystanders, but active participants in designing and implementing solutions to the difficult social problems so many of us face today and which threaten the social fabric of our communities.*

MY GOOD OLD DAYS

I grew up in the 1950s on a small dairy farm in Western New York, outside of a town with a population smaller than Hope Meadows. My grandparents lived next door, and after my grandmother died when I was six years old, my grandfather joined us—my mom, dad, sister, brother and me—for dinner every night. In this farm community, people worked hard all week long. Most families went to church every Sunday, and many evenings they would "take a drive" to visit with neighbors, none of whom were within walking distance. Divorce was rare and jobs plentiful. In hindsight, I realize it was never a perfect world—far from it—but from my child's perspective, it seemed that our lives were good and that we all cared about one another. Many years later, Hope Meadows would feel similar to me.

I think of myself as an ordinary person. When I graduated in the early 1960s from our rural high school, it was taken for granted that I would become a mother and a teacher. I did. But I never imagined I might also become a person who would one day take on the Pentagon bureaucracy. Or that I would establish and run a nonprofit organization, create an intentional community, and advocate for children who were facing serious challenges and later for older adults, including those facing the last years of their life. I never thought that one day I would conduct research with colleagues which would expose a significant missing piece in our social safety net, or that my ordinary experiences growing up with a grandparent next door in a typical farming community would inform the makeup of this piece. And I certainly never guessed that throughout my professional career, I would almost always seem to be at odds with what was considered normal or acceptable practices or beliefs at the time, and that my work would always reflect a persistent streak of unorthodoxy. Finally, I never envisioned myself as an older adult (Can any eighteen-year-old do that?), or that in our 60's, 70's or even 80's, my generation could play a significant part in advancing the health and wellbeing of people of all ages, circumstances, abilities and needs across this country.

FROM RESEARCH TO PIONEERING A HUMAN SOLUTION

The chapters that follow tell how all this came to be.

Part One explores the dynamics of individuals and families (my own family included) as we interact with large, highly regulated and often highly impersonal social service systems. Most of the stories told are of the nine children and their foster families gathered through the ethnographic research I conducted as a professor at the University of Illinois. This research upended my thinking in so many ways as I watched families depend for their lives upon a system of social services that ultimately failed them. The insights gleaned from this time with them led me to leave my university job with a new purpose: to work with others to conceive and establish Hope Meadows. Hope would be home to children and families—families who needed much love and support. It would also be—thanks to senior activist and Grey Panther founder, Maggie Kuhn—home and extended family to a veritable workforce of caring and committed senior citizens, the people who changed everything.

Part Two tells the stories of those seniors (the name they asked to be called and, in honoring them, the name I use in referring to anyone fifty-five or older), along with those of the children and the parents who came to call Hope Meadows home during the ten years I served as its director. These stories reflect our *collective vulnerability* and they depict how, through close and caring relationships, the old, the young, and all those in between helped one another to believe in a future filled with kindness, generosity and hope.

Part Three focuses on the development of core values supporting the mission and guiding the day-to-day life of the Hope Meadows community during my tenure there. These values weren't perfectly etched into our forming documents; rather, they emerged over time and through daily life together as we saw the changes in people's lives. In the same way, three critical shifts in perspective emerged, *changing how we view family, vulnerability, and older adults.* Embracing these changes in perspective and applying them to daily life resulted in a *new paradigm* for addressing some of our most intransigent social problems, helping to fill the gap between what is and what can be.

Part Four moves beyond Hope Meadows and into the here and now, where there is growing recognition that deep connection to family, friends, and community is a fundamental human need, and also a lost art. In this final section, *Intentional Neighboring* is introduced as a proven and viable way to reweave the broken threads of our social fabric through neighborhood life. You'll meet change leaders adapting this approach to address the unmet needs for inclusion and connection of individuals living with disability or with mental illness; who are homeless or aging out of foster care; or who, like Elmer, experience declining health and wellbeing due to isolation and loneliness in old age. The last chapters offer an expanded vision for intentional neighboring across communities both new and old, including in current models of aging and long-term care. They also present an overview of emerging intentional neighboring development across the country. This challenging work has the potential to strengthen our current social safety net by adding an *essential* missing piece—ordinary people like you and me who, through intentional neighboring, have the power to heal and unite us.

No matter where you are on your life's journey, I believe that something of you will relate to the work of this book. You will get to know some wonderful people whose sometimes heartbreaking and often inspiring stories will remind you of your own capacity to care and in doing so, to make a difference. May *Neighbors* give you confidence that it is possible and even essential that every one of us—and especially our nation's older adults—be a valued part of the systems and solutions we need so desperately.

Author's Note

The stories of the people presented in this book are *their* stories, captured over a thirty-year period, primarily through informal, tape-recorded, and transcribed conversations. The transcriptions allow me to re-tell their stories, enabling their authentic voices to be heard and their emotions to be felt. Some vignettes have been retold in previously published works.

Every adult whose stories were transcribed both read and attested to their accuracy and gave me permission to use them. In many cases, names are changed to protect confidentiality, including identities of all kids and parents in Part I, all minors and birth parents in Part II and all Hope parents in Part III. Details are gleaned from over 150 hours of transcribed tape-recorded interviews; twenty-three years of weekly Hope Meadows newsletters beginning in 1995; continuous national media stories; more than fifteen years of biannual progress reports; and countless formal and informal staff reports, daily conversations, and miscellaneous pieces of information gathered during the ten years I was CEO and executive director of Hope Meadows.

Part I

NOW AND THEN, OVER AND OVER AGAIN

An enhanced social science knowledge base is required for insight and perspective on the accumulated social problems that have eroded American society.[1]

Rep. George Brown, Jr.
Chairman of the House Committee
on Science, Space, and Technology,
in "Quotable," *The Chronicle of Higher Education*

- One -

We Must Do Better

The following two chapters are about families, mine included. Most are stories taken from research which kept me up at night, and which ultimately led me to new understandings about families, vulnerability, and about older adults and their important role in the health and wellbeing of our culture. You will read real-life experiences of highly vulnerable people depending upon one particular social service program—the foster care system—revealing their hurt and disappointment as they disclose the brokenness and insufficiencies of our "systems approach" to human care. But this book is not about any one program or service area, nor is it about any one group of people in need of help. I believe that most of us have had similar experiences with broken systems, or we know and/or love someone who has—parents with dementia, families facing poverty, veterans returning from war, individuals coping with severe mental illness, children and adults living with developmental disabilities, retiring adults facing life without purpose, or grandparents raising grandchildren. Whatever your connection, these stories can help us all to think differently about what humans need most, and how we might revitalize, repair and integrate our fractured networks of support.

2020: "A CATALOGUE OF HORRORS"

Each morning I read about the chronic unfolding crises of the day. Just as often, I imagine how the caring people working within divisions and agencies in our vast network of social services must be collectively frozen in fear and frustration, knowing that somehow they must respond in new ways to old and seemingly unsolvable, unending problems.

In my own state of Illinois, for example, the Department of Children and Family Services (DCFS) published a 384-page report at the end of 2019, containing, as one headline proclaimed, "A Catalogue of Horrors."[1] Once again there were no new solutions, just the usual prescriptions: "better training of caseworkers, smarter oversight of supervisors, and smaller caseloads." The acting inspector general of DCFS lamented, *"We, Illinois, must do better."*[2] This detailed report revealed a sad and tragic truth—the state is unable to meet its mandate to keep children safe and secure from anguished and often overwhelmed family members.

When bad things happen, people usually blame people, including themselves. When things go terribly wrong in families, Nicholas Kristof and Sheryl WuDunn write in their recently published book, *Tightrope: Americans Reaching for Hope*, many of us assume that "so-called personal failures…are a result of 'bad choices' rather than problems bigger than the individual: childhood abuse, lack of knowledge, dearth of resources."[3] In her review of *Tightrope,* Sarah Smarsh adds that for the working poor today (as for many of the parents in the stories to follow) there seems to be "an undercurrent of self-hatred, in which people blame themselves for bad outcomes…."[4]

But the emotional dynamics of blame are familiar to all of us. I would guess that nearly every parent has experienced similar lapses of confidence as we live through the "terrible twos" or watch in horror as our adolescent children individuate in a wholesale rejection of every treasured rule and family value. It only gets worse when we engage unsuccessfully with the social institutions intended to help us—schools, medical systems, the courts, social welfare. My friends who are parents of children with "differences" confess to an ever-present doubt regarding their abilities as parents and advocates, a doubt that coexists alongside constant tension with and distrust of the professionals that serve them. Common challenges are multiplied when nothing's working well, when disability, trauma or addictions are tearing up a family and help from outside is needed. Self-doubt, frustration and lack of trust in the very professionals and social institutions that are there to help us creates an unholy triad of trouble. Believe me, I know—from painful, firsthand, family experience.

Most of my close friends have parents or spouses with dementia. My mother recently died from this disease, and for the last two years of her life she was living in what is considered one of the best senior living facilities in our state. It was shiny new, well maintained, and run by a committed board of directors, some of whom I knew personally. Perhaps best of all, it was located in the countryside only minutes from my home. Mom could look out on acres of open fields, just as she had done all of her life in rural New York State, and I could visit her every day.

I was thrilled when this memory care facility agreed to care for my mother, because I knew I couldn't do it myself. But it wasn't long after she moved in before I had moments of self-doubt. Did I make the right decision? Mainly, I felt let down, disappointed, and—as strong a word as it may seem—deceived. My high expectations were not being met. Care, we were told, would be individualized, addressing Mom's needs, preferences, and wants. But as I watched my mother's agitation, boredom, and sense of personal inadequacy grow, it became clear that her emotional wellbeing, especially her desire to be useful and busy, was not being addressed; and worse, her "problems" were being written off as the predictable side effects of aging with dementia. It seemed to me that the management and many staff had no real expectation of happiness for their clients; even less did they expect the men and women they cared for—at their ages and in their conditions—to want or need a sense of purpose lived out in meaningful daily relationships and activities. Like many of us, they assumed, as Dr. Atul Gawande points out in *Being Mortal*, that "once you lose your physical independence, a life of worth and freedom is simply not possible."[5]

Frustrated and disappointed to witness the empty life my mother was living, I set out to make things better. I met with management and care providers often. On occasion I'd arm myself with quotes from *Being Mortal* and especially from *What are Old People For?,* written by geriatrician Dr. William H. Thomas. Although mother's basic health and safety were not often in question, it seemed to me that the staff at this institution had no idea how to help their residents, as Dr. Thomas writes, to "awake each morning and know, in truth, that their life matters...that they are in some way contributing to the wellbeing of another."[6]

I wasn't the only one concerned. Many of the adult children of the residents I met had similar disappointments, along with many of the residents themselves and even some of the care providers working inside the facility. We knew something important was missing; we also knew we could no longer trust management to fix this. In some ways, we felt as helpless as the residents. I found myself thinking back to the research I'd conducted on parents and children in the foster care system early in my career, but now in an intensely personal way. The decade and the details were of course different, but the personal disappointment, the misconceptions, and a gross inattention to basic human need are frighteningly similar. It is out of this research and the experiences of these families that the real story of Hope Meadows begins.

THE 1980'S: "CRACK KIDS" AND CRISIS RESPONSE

It was 1982. I was teaching at the University of Illinois in Urbana-Champaign and serving as the director of an interdisciplinary program where the focus was on early childhood education and on children and families with special needs. With my friend and colleague, Dr. Martha Bauman Power (Marty), I began a research project that would change the direction of my life forever. Today it is the opioid epidemic along with domestic violence, poverty, and chronic neglect that destroy lives. In the '80's and 90's it was crack cocaine, hitting our cities nationwide with a force that left over half a million children in foster care. Many were ages three and older, often entering the system alongside their brothers and sisters—and too many to count were born with drugs in their systems. The media wrote daily on the impact of this drug epidemic. No one knew what the addiction of infants would portend as they grew up. Stories predicting worst-case scenarios headlined the news: these "crack babies" would be damaged for life, never able to make a meaningful contribution to society as adults. They would be our next lost generation.

For years, adoption specialists had drawn on child development research as a basis for establishing policies around the adoption of infants. Previously, healthy infants—mostly white—were found for families, but with the crack epidemic the picture was reversed. Rather than finding infants for families to adopt, the challenge now was to find families who would adopt these "damaged" and often older children.

As is frequently the case in a crisis, our systems were not prepared. Social services were not set up to help the growing number of parents who had lost their children to foster care establish a secure and nurturing environment so that their children could be safely returned to them. And the courts were equally unequipped to hand down large numbers of decisions to either return children home or terminate parental rights. As a result, thousands of children could not go home to live with their families; but neither could they be adopted in a timely manner. Instead, they remained in what was commonly referred to as the *quagmire of foster care.*

Over a three-year period, approximately one thousand children entered the Illinois foster care system every month. Numbers grew from approximately fourteen thousand children in the system to over fifty thousand. DCFS had to find ways to address this crisis, and especially to address the needs of these children for permanent, safe, and nurturing homes. Ideally, the children would return home; but before that could happen, effective ways had to be found to work with their highly troubled parents who were dealing with not only the devastating effects of drug use, but often with the grinding weight of poverty, violence, and mental illness.

INTO THE UNKNOWN

In the meantime, when these efforts failed, DCFS had to identify and support parents willing to adopt children they labeled as "hard-to-place." These were the children who were in the system for a long time, part of a sibling group, older, or living with a medical condition, physical disabilities, emotional problems, or intellectual disabilities that made finding adoptive homes difficult. To provide this support, DCFS needed to learn how bonding could be achieved between prospective adoptive parents and children who had spent the very earliest years of their lives in foster care homes, in dysfunctional biological homes, and sometimes even in institutions. This was all new territory for them.

As an adoptive parent myself, and as someone whose interest and research had always focused on vulnerable children and families, I was intensely curious about the children in foster care who needed adoptive homes. I wanted to know who the children were—the ones who would not be returned home—and I wanted to know who the prospective adoptive parents were. I wanted to know how these children who had endured so much trauma could be successfully integrated into a new family with its own past, and how these prospective parents and these traumatized children would forge a new future together, creating a shared adoptive family story.

I learned that DCFS was about to start its first recruiting effort and training program for prospective adoptive parents. Since my research interests overlapped with their need to better understand non-infant adoptions, Marty and I were given permission to sit in and tape-record all training sessions. It was agreed that we would interview the parents and follow them as children were placed in their home, as they got to know these children, and as they made the decision whether or not to adopt.

DCFS began their training classes and placement of children while still inexperienced and overwhelmed with the crack cocaine crisis and its impact on families. I began my research with personal experience related to adoption and with an academic background in child development. But I was incredibly naïve and uninformed when it came to understanding foster care policies and practices. Consequently, as DCFS and I began this new endeavor together, neither of us could have foreseen what was about to unfold.

ALL THE WRONG ASSUMPTIONS

Marty and I began by closely following the first ten families DCFS accepted into their new adoption program. Our plan was to visit these families in their homes before any children were placed with them, then again at the time of placement, and finally, multiple times after the children were placed up until the adoptions were finalized. As the study progressed, we were increasingly involved with seven of the families, talking and meeting with them frequently and informally in a variety of settings. Two of the original families had withdrawn their request from DCFS, and a child was never placed in a third.

Nearly all of my initial assumptions about the parents turned out to be wrong. I expected that many of the families would look like mine after we adopted our son—biracial with professional parents. I expected many would live in our University town. Instead, this is what we found: all of the families were white, working-class, and from small towns. They did not want to adopt an infant because they felt that an older child, even one with a minor disability, would be less work and impinge less on their jobs than "starting over with diapers." All of the parents made it clear they did not want children over eleven years old, nor were they willing to accept black children, maintaining that they would not fit in with the community. And much to our surprise, all of the families already had children. They were not adopting for religious or social reasons, but for personal reasons, to extend or balance their families by gender or age.

If necessary, they were willing to accept children with minor medical conditions, but *every* parent said they did not want the extra responsibility to care for a child who was blind or who needed to use a wheelchair. They had specific ideas about what it might mean to parent a child with these visible conditions. One father said his family loved outdoor sports and thought a child in a wheelchair or one who was blind just would not fit in. Not so visible and of less concern to all of the parents were the emotional scars their children might carry into the home—the scars of abuse, neglect, and chronic stress. A loving home seemed a sufficient antidote.

When the adoption classes ended, the parents were excited and optimistic. Social workers had listened to them, and soon they would be getting the child or children they had been waiting for. Their families would be complete. They knew it would take time for the children to adjust, but they believed that with lots of love the kids would fit in. When they were told stories about children who might start a fire in the house or kill a family pet and nail it to the garage door, the parents remained unconcerned. Presented with these worst-case scenarios, they could not imagine such things would ever happen to them. Thankfully, they were right about that; but they were painfully mistaken regarding many other assumptions they held about life with a new child as they moved forward to extend their families through adoption.

FAILED EXPECTATIONS

We gathered the stories of these families for almost three years. Over that time nine children were placed with them: all white, physically healthy, and ranging from twenty-two months to eleven years of age. Six of the nine children each had lived in at least three different foster homes and two had spent time in institutional care. All had experienced little or no stability in their young lives.

Only a few parents expected the adoption to make major changes in their lives. They didn't anticipate any significant obstacles to falling in love with their child or to adjusting to a new person in their home. One mother told us, "I keep hoping that we're going to have a child that's maybe going to have a little problem at first, but something that will be really easy to take care of, and we will start being a family as soon as possible."[7] Other parents agreed with one dad who described the future adjustment as nothing more than "just having another kid."

But they were largely disappointed and in the end, deeply hurt. I believe that *three key expectations* held by these parents—when not realized—led rapidly to their disillusionment and ultimately to the return of most of the children back into that quagmire of foster care, further away than ever from any hope of finding a permanent, caring family and a place they could, with confidence, call home.

Love at First Sight

We humans seem to be wired to believe in love, especially when it comes to children, and especially when they are vulnerable. Our foster parents were no different, even though they knew ahead of time that the children they would be adopting were… complicated. Both moms and dads fully expected to fall in love with the kids placed with them—almost immediately. When this did not happen, they were racked with self-doubt and guilt, and grew anxious about the lack of positive feelings for their children. One mother confessed, "I wasn't warming up the way I thought I should be,"[8] and another, three weeks after her son arrived, admitted the same.

> The most disquieting thing is that I'm not in love with this child yet. I hoped I would feel something, that I would begin to feel something. See, I thought I would be attracted to this cute lovable child, you know, and I'd feel tender because he's been through so much. I expected some sort of attraction, but I don't feel that even.... I'm irritated at myself for not being able to feel like his mother.[9]

The loss of confidence in themselves as loving parents led to anxiety, discomfort, fear of failure, and disappointment in themselves and often their children. The failed expectation of instant love created nothing but pain for both parent and child.

Shared Family Values and Behaviors

Adding to the parents' disillusionment was the expectation that the kids would readily and willingly exhibit key family values including displaying age-appropriate responsibilities, showing respect, and expressing affection. But they were simply not equipped to do so. Research has shown that universal family values are best instilled when we are very young. Parents share hugs with their children and begin to teach them to say please and thank you at a very early age. Over time these acts become so ingrained that we all take them for granted. But how could these kids be expected to demonstrate such behaviors in everyday relationships when they had never or rarely experienced them?

Neglected children are simply not taught such things—no one shows them how to properly brush their teeth once they reach a certain age, or how to behave appropriately at the dinner table—what dinner table? When one has never been shown respect, how is that person expected to know what it means? And when one has rarely seen or experienced displays of affection, but instead has lived daily in a violent or neglectful environment, experiencing abandonment and disregard, how can that child be expected to express warmth, love, or joy in a relationship?

One father told us, "I just assumed that when we got Bryan, we'd be able to tell him things and he'd do it. We'd tell him not to lie but he wouldn't stop." Baffled, he went on to say, "Bryan doesn't know how to hug…he's like a board, just as stiff as a board. He just hangs there."[10]

It doesn't matter what people tell us, when there is nowhere for it to land.

Collaboration with the State

Perhaps the greatest disappointment to the parents was the failed expectation of partnership with the State of Illinois. They believed from the beginning that DCFS and its social workers would collaborate with them in the placement of children in their homes, and that this partnership would continue after the children arrived and until the adoptions were finalized. But as soon as the training classes were over, the parents realized they had little choice in the decision as to which child would be placed in their home. One mother said this:

> I think DCFS discouraged us from making a decision about who we wanted to adopt. They want to make that decision. They have all the information, and they call us when they think they have a child that fits our home. Then we get to make the decision whether we want to pursue that child or not. We're presented with a particular child over the telephone. I think that it puts a lot of discretion in the hands of the social worker. There is no way to complain; there is no person to complain to

> because the power of whether or not we get a child ever is totally in the hands of the social worker.[11]

Another father was equally concerned. "If you say no to a child," he said, "then you have to go back to square one, and who knows when the hell they'll get around to presenting another child to you."[12] These parents were afraid that they would not be given another chance, so *all* took the first child offered to them.

Social workers saw the placement process differently. When we asked a DCFS worker how these decisions were made she replied, "We leave it a lot to the families."[13] From the perspective of most case managers and social workers, families had plenty of say in the matter: they could always say "no" to a referral. The state never forced a parent to take a child; the parents were the final decision-makers.

The opposing perceptions of parents and social workers created even more problems as the placement process unfolded, leading to an almost total lack of trust once the children were in the home. The parents desperately needed help to understand and manage their children's behaviors. What, for example, should they do when their child talked back, lied, or refused to take a bath? The parents themselves had been spanked as children when they misbehaved, and some of them remembered having their mouths washed with soap for telling a lie. These disciplinary techniques, some believed, were not harmful—and they worked. But they didn't dare say that out loud, fearing their social workers might get the wrong idea, or judge them to be bad—even abusive parents—and take their children away.

In discussing this issue with the DCFS adoption coordinator, we heard something similar. She said social workers knew parents were having problems, but they felt unable to help because the parents would not confide in them as long as DCFS had the ultimate power to remove the children from their homes. DCFS' very real authority coupled with the parents' perceived lack of power formed a huge wedge between them, hampering the development of a successful partnership based on trust and effective communication. Ultimately this divide prevented the unfolding of successful adoption stories filled with empathy, compassion, and kindness.

The failed expectations from the DCFS preadoption training classes were even more pronounced in the adoption stories of two families which, each for a different reason, deeply affected me. Even today, some thirty years later, when I think of these families and the children they had hoped to adopt, a wave of deep sadness engulfs me.

- Two -

The Rules are the Rules

> Love is not only an intuition, but also a skill.[1]
>
> —Andrew Solomon, *Far from the Tree*

The stories of the Johnson and the Sheppard families are about our capacity to be and do good and what gets in the way of that; they are about systems and differentials of power and who we can trust to help us. They are stories told by ordinary people, people like you and me. The experiences they reveal are both visionary and cautionary tales for our own futures.

I had always prided myself on separating my work from my home life, leaving behind emotions that had bubbled up during the workday as I came home to spend the evening with my family. In graduate school, while doing an internship at a highly regarded children's diagnostic center, I was told never to get emotionally involved. Work was work; it was no place for emotions. Family life was just the opposite; family life was supposed to be filled with emotions. I was taught that work life and family life could not be allowed to overlap, but of course we know it is often not humanly possible to separate the two. They are always connected, as Marty and I would soon discover.

THE SHEPPARD FAMILY

Dave and Sue Sheppard wanted to adopt an older brother for their eight-year-old daughter. When ten-year-old John was presented to them, they readily agreed to have him placed in their home. DCFS provided them with considerable information about his past. His mother was eighteen when he was born. She never married or maintained a relationship with his father. John was hospitalized before he was two for failure to thrive. Soon after, his mother married a man who, for two years, beat both her and her son. Finally she left, taking John with her, but it wasn't long before they moved in with another man who also beat John and sexually abused him. At age six, John was removed from this home to spend two years in an institution for children with emotional and behavioral problems, after which he was placed in a series of foster homes followed by a second institution. When John was ten, parental rights were terminated, and he went to live with the Sheppards, who adopted him one year later.

Like other children in our study, John had difficulty taking responsibility, lacked respect for adult authority, and was emotionally unresponsive. The Sheppards knew about John's past; still, they believed they would have little trouble parenting him. But they did have problems, which Dave attributed to the time John spent in institutions:

> The biggest thing is the day-to-day lack of responsibility for anything. And that's basically institutionalization as

> we see it. He has no respect for adults at all. He talks back. He will not do anything we tell him to do unless he is absolutely forced to do it. He refuses to change his underwear unless we stand there and force him; he won't make his bed. We spend three hours in an evening forcing this kid to do his homework…and then he won't bother to hand it in.[2]

John's behaviors didn't change, and the Sheppards needed help: "Frustration marks every attempt we make to teach John our family ways."[3] Despite this, they were the first family in our study to adopt. But not long after they had adopted John, both Dave and Sue told us they did not feel like they were his father or mother, both of them admitting, "We do not love him."[4] In the end, a tragic episode occurred which precipitated their decision to terminate their parental rights. They told us this story:

> We'd had a day where John was avoiding more responsibility than usual. It was Saturday morning; he was doing dishes, doing them over again from the previous night because they weren't clean. That's the way we started the morning. From there on I had to ask John several times if he'd made his bed.
>
> He said 'Yes,' he had made his bed.
>
> 'Are you sure? If I go up there, will I be angry?'
>
> 'No, I made my bed; you are going to be happy.'
>
> 'Fine,' I said. So, I go upstairs to check out everything else, and John's bed has not been made. Unsurprised, I raised my voice, 'Don't argue with me, just make it!'
>
> And then he shoots me a hateful glance, and…looks at me with a you-should-be-dead—what-the-hell-are-you-

> doing-alive-woman look. So I balled up my fist, and I put it to his cheek. I was shaking; I was furious, and I was telling him that he was going to do what I said or else!
>
> Dave was standing two feet away. He shouted at me, 'Sue, no!'
>
> I had my hand against John's cheek; I'm really angry; I'm still shaking, and I pushed his head with my hand, so that his head is tilted up against the wall, and I wanted to hit him; oh God, I wanted to hit him. In fact, in my mind, I could visualize that if I hit him, there would be blood on the floor.
>
> Dave begged me, 'Don't hit him!'
>
> 'But I want to hit him!' I screamed, 'I want to hit him! I want to hurt him!' Dave dragged me off...I was crying at this point, sobbing, 'I can't help it; I just hate him! I really do hate him!'[5]

Within days the Sheppards called their child welfare contact to begin proceedings: *they wanted to give up all rights to parent John.* To ensure John's removal from their home, the Sheppards felt pressed to convince the court that he could not safely stay in their family—or in any family. They had to portray his behaviors as deviant enough to justify their surrender of him. In essence, they told the judge that no one could ever feel safe as long as John was in their home. They said he might sexually assault children or go after adults with a knife. Whether or not these predictions were fair or accurate is unclear, but the court certainly took them into consideration when making its ruling.

Now twelve years old, John was sent for the third time in his life to an institution for emotionally and behaviorally disturbed children. Soon after he was removed from their home, the Sheppards received a letter: "I love you," John wrote. "I will kill myself to go back to you. If I go to another family, I will kill myself for sure. Please bring me back. I will try better."[6]

Sue didn't know how to respond to John's plea, so she called a DCFS caseworker who suggested that she and Dave answer John in a letter describing *what he did* and why they terminated the adoption. Instead, the letter they wrote expressed their own sense of failure: "We realized that we were not teaching you about love or about how a family should share concern, responsibility, and caring. We were not happy, and we were not helping you. We were afraid we would hurt you more if you stayed than if you left our family."[7]

Several years later Sue spoke honestly about the pain:

> When John came to live with us we expected…adjustments and difficulties, but we imagined those adjustments would be similar to ones we had experienced in our pasts. We had a nescient faith that we would be able to adjust and overcome any problems simply because we were compassionate adults, and we wanted so much for this adoption to work. We could not begin to imagine the difficulties of reconciling our vastly different worlds of experience.[8]

JOHN AND MY SON

The Sheppards' experience was heart-wrenching for everyone involved, but especially for John. All of the families in our study experienced disappointment, frustration, and, yes, anger at times. But the Sheppards were the only family to adopt and then undo the adoption. Marty and I went to court the day their parental rights were terminated. Prior to this, it had never ever entered my mind that once an adoption was finalized, it could be undone. Since I was not aware that adoptive parents could terminate their parental rights, I was stunned that such a proceeding was even taking place and only weeks after the Sheppards had requested it! Sitting in the courtroom, I could only think of John. A million questions raced through my mind. *What did he really do to deserve this? What must he be thinking and feeling? What would happen to him now? How often did this happen to other families?* And finally, *would this have happened if John had been the Sheppard's biological son; would the court have made the same decision?*

Then I thought of my son. Wayland and I adopted Seth when he was eighteen months old. He is now well into middle adulthood and will be the first to say that for a few of his late adolescent and young adult years, our relationship was not always the smoothest. But during those years, to not be his legal parents, for him not to be our son—that was unimaginable!

But I also knew that to compare the Sheppards to our family was not entirely fair. While John had lived the first ten years of his troubled life before meeting the Sheppards, our son Seth—after his first eighteen months of life—was always a part of our family story. Our daily lives together provided us with the context we needed to understand one another. But Sue's life history was so unlike her adopted son's past that it seemed they had come from different worlds. She simply could not understand him, nor could she accept the complexities of his past and how it impacted their lives. She wanted and expected things that John could not deliver—and instead he did things that she and her husband did not expect and could not accept. Without the benefit of a shared family story, misunderstandings grew into continual frustration and disappointment.

I could see that this same "disconnect" occurred as social service workers, lawyers, caregivers and program administrators tried to help other families in our study to build a positive future with their new children. Another unholy triad of trouble emerged as children, new parents, and institutional professionals—all with very different histories and perspectives, tried to work things out efficiently and expeditiously, by the book and according to expectations, often with terrible results and much pain.

As I sat in that courtroom, I knew how inconceivable it would be for me to see Seth go through such a painful experience, one that would change and scar his life forever. If it was unthinkable to imagine the anguish, confusion, rejection, and heartache such experiences would engender in my own son, then there had to be a way to prevent this from happening to other adopted children. It was too late for John and his adoptive parents, but surely something could be done to prevent others from enduring such pain and loss—others, who, like John and the Sheppards, were living an adoption story in which their daily lives were filled with feelings of helplessness, hopelessness, and despair. There just had to be a way.

THE JOHNSONS

Like the Sheppard's, Dick and Pat Johnson's adoption story was also filled with frustration and disillusionment. But unlike the Sheppards, the Johnsons were not challenged by the behaviors of a highly troubled child, but rather by DCFS and the entanglements of birthparents as they tried to adopt Sam—a boy who cared for everyone.

Sam's mother had serious mental health issues for which she was frequently hospitalized. His father had problems with alcohol, and both parents had physical disabilities. As a result, neither was able to cope with parenting an active, intelligent young child. When he was six, Sam was removed from his parents' care and placed in a foster home. Over the next two years he moved from this foster home, back to his parents' home, into a second foster home, and then to the home of an aunt and uncle. Beth and David were caring and concerned relatives, but they had three teenage children, and after a year decided they could not commit to adopting Sam. Then almost eight, Sam was placed in the home of Pat and Dick, whose son Jake was four years old.

All the while, Sam's birthparents were still trying to get him back. When Sam was first removed from his birthparents, they were given a year to correct situations in their home in order to have Sam returned to them. After the year was over, this court order was extended for another year. During this two-year period Sam had weekly home visits, each lasting for approximately two hours. A "homemaker" was assigned to Sam by DCFS to transport and accompany him during visits with his parents and then return him to his temporary home with his aunt and uncle.

The Johnsons first met Sam by going with a social worker to Sam's relatives' home. There was immediate rapport between the two couples. They arranged for Sam to visit one day with Pat and Dick and return to Beth and David in the evening. A week later he moved in with the Johnsons. When we asked Pat what her first thoughts were when she met Sam she said, "He was like his picture. He was very talkative.... It was like that... for the first few days. You both are not like the way you usually are. You want him to be happy and he is trying to impress you and back and forth."[9] Once Sam moved in with the Johnsons, the court continued to give his birthparents the opportunity to get him back. When Pat learned that Sam's parents were required to demonstrate to DCFS that they could fix a meal and take Sam to the park, she complained:

> It doesn't make any sense when you first think about it. Sam is going to go there and stay overnight, which to me is a bunch of baloney. The parents have [already] proved they can't handle it. DCFS says the reason they are doing this is to have a stronger case when they go to court. Why are they dragging it on so long? This is what makes me so mad, and it makes me mad at DCFS because, you know, you can't blame Sam for feeling like he doesn't belong. Hopefully they will get this thing in court and get it settled one way or the other. Not knowing if we are going to get to keep Sam [makes me] afraid to get as close to him as I would like to.[10]

Sam's understanding of what his parents had to do in order for him to go home to them permanently differed from Pat's. He told us they had to learn "how to scold me right," and added, "When I was there, when I did something, I'd get a whooping, only it wasn't real soft. It hurt. One day I got one with a belt, and I got blisters…." Sam paused, remembering, and then continued, "and there is another reason why they have to be ready… 'cause they can get drunk on wine…and my dad tried to kill my Mom."[11]

Sam told us about the time both parents were drunk and he "called the operator and called the police."[12] This incident precipitated his removal from his parents' home and into the foster care system, something for which he felt largely responsible.

Sam lived with the Johnsons for fourteen months when Pat took him for a scheduled visit with his parents at a DCFS office. Pat described what happened afterward.

> Sam came out and he was so upset and mad and it just so happened that we had to go to mental health after that. On the way over there, Sam said, 'I'm really mad.'

I asked him, 'What are you mad about?'

Sam said his Mom wanted him to kiss and hug her and he didn't want to. 'When the guy came back in the room, Mom told him that I wouldn't do what she wanted.'

I told Sam to just let it go. It was not something to get so upset about. Then he told me that his parents were… cutting Dick and I down, and they were saying we were not good, our rules were not good, and we were mean because he had to play by himself sometimes.

Once we [Sam, Pat and Dick] arrived at the mental health office, we talked to the therapist.

Sam was really upset. 'I feel like I'm being torn apart,' he said. 'I have one set of parents here telling me one thing and this set of parents telling me something else. And, I don't want to take sides.… I know that you and Dick do love me and that what you are doing is right. But how can I tell my Mom and Dad because I don't want to make them mad?'

And so I explained, 'You have to understand. We have you with us. They want to have you with them and they can't. And so of course they are mad so that is how they are taking it out.'

That night Sam came to me, and said, 'Mom, I want to say something. I want to thank you for telling me the truth.'[13]

Ten months later Sam's parents' rights still had not been terminated. Dick was adamant about keeping Sam in their family: "I'm in this thing and I'm sticking this thing out, and I'm going to win the battle with Sam no matter what it takes. You don't take kids and pawn them like they're some item in a store. We've come a long way. Just because something happens you don't send a kid off. Jake does something; I don't get rid of *him*."

Dick went on to tell us that the day before, Sam said, "It just seems like my real parents don't care about me." When Dick asked why he thought such a thing, Sam replied, "They won't do anything they are supposed to do." Sam also told Dick that he did not want to be adopted if it would mean he could never see his mom and dad again.

Dick understood: "He wants contact with his parents to know that they're all right. But I told him that [our adopting him] does not mean he can't see his parents: I think after knowing we would let him have contact, he feels better."[14]

Dick truly believed that soon there would be enough evidence to terminate parental rights. But not long after this interview, Sam was visited at school by an investigator from DCFS. Someone had dialed the hotline the day before to report that six weeks prior they had observed two finger marks—bruises—on Sam's neck. Sam was taken from the school to a DCFS office and then driven by a DCFS homemaker to a scheduled visit with his parents. He later told Dick and Pat that on the ride there, the homemaker admitted to filing the report.

The next day, the Johnsons met with Sam's teacher at school, who said she had never seen any marks on Sam except for some scratches made by their dog and cat. She told the Johnsons, "Sam is such an outgoing person that if something had happened to him, he would surely come in and tell us about it."

Pat called a social worker that day to report that Sam was frustrated and angry because DCFS refused to believe him when he insisted over and over that they (Pat and Dick) had never done a thing to hurt him. Spanking, Sam believed, was not wrong.

Sam knew that when he got a spanking, he deserved a spanking. And I told that to the lady on the phone! It was funny. She sat there and said, 'I agree that children need spankings, but the law is you don't spank them.'

I told her, 'You are saying one thing and then turning around and saying something else.'

DCFS eventually called to say they were keeping the report of abuse in the Johnson's file. Dick believed they made this decision because, "They disliked us. We were too close to Sam's relatives," and through them, "we knew too much that was not complimentary to DCFS."

Pat was more matter-of-fact. She believed the DCFS decision was not based on the hotline call *per se*; but rather on the fact that the Johnsons had once washed Sam's mouth out with soap for lying and that occasionally they spanked him, just as they did with Jake when he did something wrong. Pat said she never spanked hard enough to leave marks, and Sam's teacher reported that she had told DCFS exactly what she had told Pat and Dick: she had never seen a mark on Sam that indicated abuse.

We asked Pat to tell us what happened when the social worker telephoned to confirm that the report of abuse would remain on their record. It was a devastating conversation:

I [Pat] was in shock. 'You say that we are abusing Sam, but yet you can leave him in my house for four days? What are you going to do with him now?'

The social worker answered, 'Well, we'd like to come out and talk to you.'

'No. I'm beyond talking. You've accused me; you've

lied to me; but we haven't done anything. I'm not taking any more,' I said, and then I asked her, 'What is your decision?'

All the woman said to me was, 'Well, with all the strain and all the legal problems and everything that has been put on your family, it would probably be best to move him.'

I couldn't believe it, but I said, 'Fine, you pick him up at 3:00.'

'Well, we don't do things this way,' she told me.

But I was really upset and I said, 'I'm sorry. I don't want him to go, but I haven't done what you've accused me of. I'm not putting up with any more. I am finished.'

The worker came to our home at 2:45 p.m., just as Dick was leaving to pick up Sam from school. She said to me, 'I thought I would come a few minutes early. I need information for the parent termination review Friday.'

I was furious. 'You've got to be kidding,' I said. 'You want information from me after what you've done? I'm not giving you any. You have not done Sam fair! What you've accused me of…you know darn good and well that the homemaker is mad because we turned her in for stealing; we turned her in for other stuff too, so this is her way of getting back. If she was concerned, why didn't she go to your office that day or the next day and report the finger marks, and then you could have come out and seen Sam and had your evidence right then and there? Why are you waiting for a month?'

'The homemaker had nothing to do with this,' she said to me. 'We don't know that it was her.'

'Don't sit there and lie to me,' I said. 'You've done it

> enough. Two people have said it was her. She told Sam [herself] and Susan (the DCFS supervisor) told us that it was the homemaker! You can lie to yourself but don't lie to me.'
>
> The worker just looked at me and said, 'Well I'm sorry that you feel this way. You're being very immature.'
>
> 'How would you act,' I asked her, 'if somebody accused you of beating a child? Now I suppose my name can be mud…well, here's my license, I don't want to see you again. I want nothing to do with your office. I'm done!'

When Sam came into the house, the DCFS worker informed him that he would be leaving the Johnson home immediately. Pat said he bawled and screamed, repeating over and over, "I don't want to go."

At this point, both Pat and Dick were incredulous, angry, and upset. They told the social worker that taking Sam away was child abuse—that he would never recover. To which, according to Pat, the social worker sat calmly in their living room and explained, "The rules are the rules; there is nothing you can do; there is nothing we can do; we just follow them."[15]

A TURNING POINT

I arrived home from this meeting with the Johnsons in late afternoon. Wayland was busy starting dinner. Our daughter, Sarah, who was the same age as Sam, came running out to greet me, full of joy and eager to tell me about her day at school. I gave her a big hug and listened to her stories. I could not imagine how terrified she would be if a stranger came to our door and told her she had to leave her family and move to the home of people she had never met. She would leave not knowing if she would ever see us again.

Such an experience would be worse than child abuse—I couldn't even put a name to it.

How could this happen to any child? And why to Sam? He was so deeply concerned that something would happen to his birthparents because of their multiple problems; he felt guilty because he had called the police and then he had been taken away; and he wanted so much to not be in a position where he felt "torn apart."

As with John, I was profoundly affected by what had happened to Sam. John and our son had something in common: both were adopted. Sarah and Sam had something in common too. They were not only the same age; they shared the same birthday!

Two dynamics were at play resulting in the Johnsons being constantly frustrated and very often angry—*unmet expectations and unequal power relationships*. Pat and Dick never expected to become enmeshed in the foster care system; they simply wanted to adopt a child. But the expressed goal of DCFS was that Sam be returned home to his birthparents, not that he be adopted. No one could win. Sam was torn between wanting to be with his mom and dad as well as wanting to stay with the Johnsons. Pat and Dick wanted and needed an agency relationship where the people they worked with could help them understand the complexities of both DCFS decision making and of Sam's parents who were deeply troubled. And the caseworkers had to follow rules. They were given an impossible job within an overwhelmed, understaffed, and underfunded agency.

The system was broken. Rules and day-to-day realities were not in sync. Like the Sheppards and the Johnsons, I, too, had had enough. I could no longer continue to be the impartial researcher who gathered stories, interpreted them within a theoretical framework, and published the results in academic journals. I really believed that most—but not all—DCFS workers did the best they could, as did the parents and these children who had experienced so much trauma. But it wasn't enough.

I didn't know what I could do to change things, but from the day I left the Johnson's house for the last time, I knew I had to try to do something. I read and read again the transcripts of the parents' voices from our study, while continually thinking about what would be best for my own two children. Soon, with some persistence and more than a little luck, the germ of an idea began to take shape. It was an out-of-the-ordinary idea, and not a simple one. But, as the Bill and Melinda Gates Foundation claim on their website: "We can't do the same things the same way and make progress."[16]

WALKING IN THEIR SHOES

During these past few years spent caring for my mother, I found myself strongly relating to the families I had studied so many years earlier. I was walking in their shoes, no longer an impartial researcher, but now as a person dependent on people in power to meet needs when I simply could not. Although I had lost faith in the senior care community where my mom lived, I knew moving her would cause chaos and fear in her life. Over time, I gave up trying to make a difference (some would call it complaining) for fear they would ask my mom to leave. How like the parents who took the first child offered to them out of fear they would never be chosen again! I loved my mother dearly, but one minute I'd feel guilty about not providing the very best for her, and the next minute I was resentful of the time it took to manage her care. She had made such sacrifices for me and for our family throughout her life, and I knew one day soon I would miss her deeply. Much like the parents in our study, I was fighting two battles: one with myself and the other with the service system that was failing my mother.

It is an irony that the responsibilities of our systems of social services are greater than ever before, and yet, as Yuval Levin, a scholar at the American Enterprise Institute observes, we are "living through a social crisis which has followed a collapse of our confidence in institutions."[17] And, as the experiences of the Sheppards and the Johnsons, (and of the current state of our political life) help us to know, the result of our deep distrust in institutions to fulfill their obligation to help us leads to a loss of mutual respect, of dignity and of hope. Ultimately not only do individuals and families suffer, so too do our social service systems and our nation.

- Three -

Power, Politics and Persistence

> What the best and wisest parent wants for his own child, that must the community want for all its children.[1]
>
> —John Dewey, *The School and Society*

After our research was completed, I could nonetheless not stop thinking about the children and the parents who had shared so much of themselves with Marty and me. What these families needed were professionals whom they could trust and easily talk to. The professionals involved needed expertise in working with children who had serious emotional problems. Personal experience related to adoption also would have helped immensely.

Working with these families, agency professionals had to understand that to be successful they had three main responsibilities: first, to become compassionate and discerning listeners in order to gain confidence and trust; second, to provide both helpful and practical advice as well as emotional support to validate the parents' feelings and experiences; and third, to make at least one social worker available to families on a consistent, frequent basis and over an extended period of time. For these things to happen, much would need to change within our system of child protective services, as explained to us during many of our conversations with DCFS personnel.

Far too often social workers felt their hands were tied due to situational constraints, including extensive caseloads, staff turnover and shortages, lack of knowledge about the parents or the children, and the pressure to place children in pre-adoptive homes as quickly as possible. One social worker admitted,

> We don't get to know the kids as much as we should. A lot of times we don't even get the kids transferred [from the foster care unit to the adoption unit] until parental rights are terminated, and then sometimes you rely on another agency, or another institution, or on foster parents and what they have told you. So, we're weighing all these things…we're doing all this matching and all this placement, and a lot of it from a piece of paper.[2]

Another social worker who had placed two kids with one of the families had only been with DCFS for a short period of time:

> I didn't study the family…I did not participate in any of the discussion groups, so I was at a disadvantage. I was relying on what others said in the group meetings and then reading what had already been written about the family. A lot of times you are under this deadline or pressure; you want to move the kids and so you're saying and collecting this stuff, and they seem like a good family… so sometimes you go with that.[3]

The children were also at a disadvantage. They rarely, if ever, had an opportunity to talk to other kids who were in the foster care system. Nor did they feel free to talk to their birth or foster/pre-adoptive parents, and they had no social worker with whom they could have developed a trusting, caring relationship. This was primarily due to staff turnover and separate social workers in the foster care and adoption divisions of DCFS. The end results were young children completely isolated by the system seeking to serve their needs, with no one to turn to when they most needed caring, trustworthy people in their lives.

To meet all the needs of the parents and the children seemed to me an impossible task. I kept thinking about the Sheppards and the Johnsons, about John and Sam, about all the families in our study. I began to think the situation was hopeless, that there really wasn't anything I, or frankly anyone, could do that would make a significant difference. The weeks and months dragged on; finally one day after I had been on vacation with my family for two weeks, it came to me: I had to let go of DCFS rules and practices and think about how to build a new support system for pre-and post-adoptive parents, the children—and for the birth families when possible. *I had to wipe the slate clean and start from scratch.*

WHAT DO ALL FAMILIES NEED?

Free to dream without the confines of rules and regulations, I let my mind wander and began to ask myself, What if? What if the unthinkable happened? In what might seem like the blink of an eye, what if Wayland and I perished in a plane crash or car accident, leaving our children without the security of our love—without any sense of wellbeing? What if there were no relatives to take on the responsibility of parenting them? Ideally, friends of ours—a family our children had grown up with—would take on this responsibility either through adoption or guardianship. This family would be there for our kids, not just until they turned eighteen, but always. Still, this would not be enough. I knew this family would need both professional support and peer support in helping our kids learn to live with this terrible loss, no less than Sarah and Seth themselves. And as I walked through our neighborhood, I thought how important it was to us. We all need community. I wanted for my kids a neighborhood that was diverse. I especially did not want a neighborhood where every child was or had been in foster care, or where every child had lost parents. I didn't want a neighborhood where all families were roughly the same age. Children, I believed—and society—benefitted from diversity.

I began to see that I wanted to create a small community of people to support families like the Sheppards and the Johnsons. I would find approximately twelve families who wanted to adopt children from the foster care system. They would live as neighbors so they could support each other and the kids would not feel isolated. I wanted most of the families to already have some biological or adopted children so that it was not just a neighborhood of children from foster care. And I wanted a very small staff that would be in the neighborhood *every day* to support the parents and the children, to be their advocates, mentors, and friends.

Now—*How do I begin to make this happen?*

When I thought about what my children need, about what all children and families need, answers to my questions began to fall into place. But how was I going to take these "answers" and make them a reality, not for my children, please God, but for the oh so many young children like John and Sam who desperately needed a deeply nurturing, loving family and a strong caring neighborhood? Answers to this question proved to be far more elusive, leading frequently to frustration and even despair. But I had to persist.

First, I needed to establish a nonprofit organization as I knew that one day I would need financial support for this neighborhood. As luck would have it, I connected with a local physician who had formed her own 501c3 with friends in Chicago—Hope for the Children. Its mission was related to adoption, but it had not been active for several years. Soon I became the executive director of this already established nonprofit and a new board was formed. I became we.

Next, we needed to find and secure land and housing. We had no money, nor did any of us have any background in housing. To compensate, we hoped to find one or two people with power who would be advocates for my idea and who would help Hope for the Children find money for the land and housing. The president of the university where I worked had been recently named as the most powerful person in Champaign-Urbana, but I thought it doubtful that he would help us.

The second most powerful person on the list was John Hirschfeld, a prominent attorney who was active in local, state, and national politics. I knew that John, through his law practice, facilitated adoptions, but I knew little else except that he was a highly controversial public figure. His political beliefs were completely different than my own, but he *was powerful*, I thought, so what did I have to lose? I called to make an appointment with him and within a few days found myself in his office. I told him about my research findings and about my ideas for creating a small caring community. He was stern, but he listened respectfully and then said simply, "Come back when you have something more."

HOPE ACCORDING TO JOHN

John was full of mischief. I smile every time I read his version of our first meeting, as told to Wes Smith in his book entitled *Hope Meadows.* I'm certain I would have never said some of the things he attributes to me. But that was John:

> When Brenda first sat down in my office and started telling me about her plans, I thought, 'Oh horseshit, here we go again, another flaming liberal with a pie-in-the-sky concept.' It was an interesting confrontation. She's a liberal Democrat. I'm a conservative Republican.
>
> Brenda told me up front that she just wanted to use my experience and contacts. She said she had never voted for me, and that she never liked me much based on what she'd read and heard about me. I thought, 'I sort of like this woman.' She was no shrinking violet. I don't like people who are easily intimidated. Still, I intended only to talk with her a little while and then kick her out of my office, saying I was retired from politics and didn't have the clout she thought I had. But as she talked, I got intrigued. I'd throw a barb out and she'd respond with something of her own.
>
> Our fifteen-minute meeting blossomed into a two-hour conversation. And into an unusual friendship. I came to see her as a visionary who was malleable—as long as you use a hammer. When Brenda came to me she had stars in her eyes and I tried to get her to be more realistic, but I was all for what she was trying to do. The law says everything is supposed to be done in the best interests of the child. But that's not how it is working.

> Brenda's concept was to provide permanency for the kids. I don't know if it will answer all the problems, but it's a step in the right direction. I told her I would do all of her legal work pro bono, but that she was going to need a lot of help politically.[4]

One year after this first meeting with John, a complete stranger called me and said she had heard I was looking for housing for adoptive families. Did I know there might be housing available at the Chanute Air Force Base, which was slated to close? The base was located in Rantoul, Illinois, about thirty minutes from where I lived. Once again, a million questions raced through my mind, from the mundane to the inconceivable: "*How will I get through the guarded gates of a military base to see this housing?*" "*How much will it cost, and where on earth will I get the money to buy it?*" And then this question: "How *could I possibly work with the Department of Defense (DoD)?*"

So, off I went to see John again. At first, like the year before, he was very stern as I started to tell him why I needed to see him. This demeanor was classic John and always made me feel a little uneasy, but I would forge ahead and eventually he would give me the smile and the twinkle in his eye that I came to so deeply appreciate. When I told him about the base housing, he immediately picked up his phone and called retired Air Force Major General Frank Elliot, the base commander. Just a few days later I found myself at Chanute being given a tour of housing that had been built for young military families who were stationed there for training.

It passed my litmus test. The housing was good enough in design and quality that under the right circumstances, I could easily see raising my children in it. I told the housing director that I needed fifteen housing units at most.

"Sorry, Brenda." she said. "The base housing will be divided into subdivisions. You'll have to take eighty units."

Eighty units! I returned to John's office and announced, "John, I want some of the Chanute housing. I need to know what to do next!"

He had the answer: "You fight the DoD; I'll take care of getting the money."

I left his office with new hope. How difficult could it be to fight the DoD, now that I had met General Elliot? (Did I mention how naïve I was?) And, I was truly relieved when John told me he would take care of finding the money. This was the task I had never been able to do! Even as an eight-year-old, I was unable to ask neighbors and friends to buy Christmas cards to benefit our local Methodist Church. To this day it's painful for me to ask individuals for money—no matter how great the need or worthy the cause. Foundations and government agencies are a different matter!

ANOTHER EPIPHANY

A big question still remained: What in the world would I do with eighty housing units when I only had use for fifteen? A chance encounter led to the answer.

A few months after meeting with John, I was in Philadelphia visiting my dear friend, Susan Martel. She told me that Maggie Kuhn, the founder of the Grey Panthers, an advocacy group of senior activists, was speaking at a local church and we needed to attend. I was not particularly interested in doing this. After all my interest was in helping children—not older adults—but I agreed to go. Maggie was in her nineties at the time. She had trouble walking, seeing, and hearing, but she could sure give a rousing talk!

Greater Philadelphia is home to a number of colleges and universities and at the time students desperately needed affordable housing. Meanwhile many of the city's older adults needed help if they were to be able to remain in the beautifully crafted old-stone homes in which they had lived for much of their adult lives. Maggie's idea was to have a student live in these houses in exchange for helping the owner with shopping, house cleaning, etc., and, to provide companionship as well. It was a brilliant idea, a win-win for everyone, and one which eventually would be replicated around the world.

On the flight home to Illinois from Philadelphia the next day, I kept thinking about the eighty housing units we would have to take and what to do with them. I wanted a *normal* neighborhood, so I was not about to fill eighty homes with children living with special needs due in part to time spent in foster care. Somewhere over Ohio the idea came to me. Maggie Kuhn's idea turned around in my mind. *Instead of students helping older adults, I would ask older active adults, for reduced rent, to help the foster/adopt parents and their children.* By the time the plane landed in Champaign, I had in my head a fully-formed plan for what would eventually become Hope Meadows.

John loved the intergenerational idea, and he kept his end of the bargain. For three years we both wrote countless letters and spent hours and hours on the phone to federal agencies all over the country. We worked closely with U.S. Senator Paul Simon, whose staff also labored tirelessly on our behalf. But the bureaucratic runaround was *endless.* One call always led to another—I alone logged over a thousand calls! Everyone knew foster care was a national crisis, everyone thought the idea had merit, and they knew that this might be a good use for some of the surplus military housing. What they did not know was how to negotiate with a nonprofit. There were no rules for this, and without rules to follow their hands were tied. The more they said they didn't know how to help me acquire the housing, the more I dug in my heels. Had one person said my idea was crazy, I might have stopped fighting, but no one ever did.

All along, John was working on getting money. In April 1993, our mutual friend and lobbyist, Betsy Mitchell, helped to introduce an appropriation request for Hope Meadows into the Illinois State budget. Two months later the budget passed and Hope was awarded one million dollars to pilot the development of our community of intergenerational support! *Still,* the Department of Defense could not imagine how to negotiate with us for surplus military housing.

Three months flew by. We had a million dollars, which then seemed to me like a hundred million today—in other words, a fortune. It was September 1993 and the base was scheduled to close in nine days; still, the DoD had not budged. I called the housing director at Chanute and through my tears, said I was ready to give up the fight.

"Not so fast," she told me, "there is one more thing we might try."

"What could that possibly be?" I asked.

"The military does not like Presidential Inquiries."

"What is a Presidential Inquiry?"

She laughed. "A request to the President of the United States asking for an investigation into a problem."

At this point I had no options left and was willing to do just about anything. I asked her to fax me a draft of an inquiry which I would then revise and send to the President. Two hours later the deed was done—a three-paragraph appeal sent to then President Clinton, reminding him that he had come into office promising to end the quagmire in government. *Well, here was one thing he could do to help keep that promise.* The only reason the DoD would not negotiate with us was because they did not have official rules on how to do so. We had hundreds of thousands of kids in foster care, many of whom needed safety and a permanent nurturing home; we had surplus housing that could help address this problem; and, we had a bureaucracy that was not allowing this to happen. In the hope of sharing my ultimate frustration, I wrote in caps, bold and underlined: THE PROBLEM ALL ALONG HAS BEEN THAT NO ONE IN THE AIR FORCE BASE DISPOSAL AGENCY HAS BEEN WILLING TO MAKE A FINAL DECISION ON ANY MATTER RELATED TO THE NEGOTIATED SALE. At the end, I asked politely, "Would you please look into this?"

After sending the inquiry, an idea occurred to me. I called the housing director, thanked her for her help, and asked one more favor. In my twenties during the Watergate scandal, I was always glued to the senate committee hearings broadcasted on radio and TV. Inspired, it occurred to me now to ask my own "Deep Throat" to leak everywhere the news of our request for a presidential intervention. She did exactly that, and then called me a week later with the news that representatives from DoD wanted to meet—immediately! Suddenly anxious to conduct negotiations before the scheduled base closing—just two days away—they definitely wanted to resolve this before the President had time to intervene.

John accompanied me to Rantoul for these negotiations. We still had no idea what the housing would cost. To John's surprise, they offered to sell us eighty housing units on twenty acres of land for $225,000! I turned to him and whispered, "We can't pay that much. It is about one quarter of all the money we have and who knows how much the renovations will cost, much less what it will cost to start the program!"

John looked at me like I was crazy—which I now admit I definitely was—and said, "Take it or you will be negotiating with the DoD for the next ten years!" I knew instantly he was probably right and *this definitely was something I could not do*! The next step seemed clear. After running on fumes and blind faith for so long, why not jump off one more cliff?

I think the DoD would agree with John about my "malleability," and maybe DCFS would too, when in the coming years we fought persistently against practices we firmly believed were not in the best interest of the children and families at Hope Meadows.

As John said, we did develop an unusual and very dear friendship. Over the next decade, before he became ill, I called on him three or four times a year when I was worn down from dealing with DCFS rules and court rulings, when I felt helpless. John always made time for me, gave me his big smile, made a phone call or two to clear up a matter, or offered some good advice. I always left his office with a smile and renewed energy, ready to face the next challenge. How wonderful and priceless these gifts of hope were.

John benefitted too. How he loved the children! He often came to Hope for holiday celebrations, and it seemed to me a child was always sitting on his lap. He had been an enormous help in the establishment of Hope Meadows. In return, when he was with the children, he experienced what I believe may have been for him rare moments of pure joy and personal fulfillment.

FROM DREAM TO REALITY

Why did I continue to be surprised at how slowly the wheels of bureaucracy work? Once negotiations for the housing were completed, it would be six more months of phone calls and a not-so-pleasant letter from John to the Secretary of the Air Force before the military would let us enter the property, nine months before the Office of the President would respond to our inquiry, and three years before the Pentagon would officially hand over the deed to the property to us.

Acquiring that deed involved a mountain of tedious paperwork, but thankfully, it did not interfere with our efforts to establish Hope Meadows. Within weeks of negotiations the board and I, as its president, began to assemble a small staff for Hope for the Children. Our overall concern was to find individuals who would excel in carrying out our vision for a new innovative model of community support for foster/adoptive families. For this, we specifically wanted staff with a streak of unorthodoxy, the ability to make tough decisions, and above all else, the skill set to build and maintain trusting and caring relationships with community residents of all ages and life experiences. They also needed to be able to stand up to DCFS when necessary. Finding people with these leadership qualities was harder than we expected. Two years later, this challenge led to my assuming the role of executive director.

Once we were given keys to our eighty housing units, we were ready to make our dream a reality. The Pentagon never once interfered as we converted twenty-four duplexes into twelve homes for pre-adoptive families and soon filled them. Along with these were forty-plus single apartment units, each eighteen hundred square feet, to be occupied by older active adults providing six hours per week of service in support of the children and families in exchange for reduced housing costs. The government's only stipulation was that until we had the deed, all housing had to be rentals only.

The years I'd spent dealing with government bureaucracy had taught me a lot, but nothing could've prepared me for the relentless rules and requirements of the State of Illinois. One of the first tasks they required was for Hope to become its own state-licensed foster care and adoption agency. As part of the licensing application, I had to write our operational philosophy, which included a list of principles related to children, seniors, and parents. This list was based on our belief that sustained and caring intergenerational relationships—parent and child, child and senior, senior and parent—are crucial elements to everyone's wellbeing. Putting our philosophy into practice would be more complicated than we could ever imagine as the implementation of our values and beliefs stood in direct opposition to standard rules and practices of our state's child welfare system. We would live in a perpetual state of frustration and aggravation and endure some painful failures as well. But Hope would be worth it as we tried (sometimes unsuccessfully) to heed the sage advice of President Franklin Delano Roosevelt: "When you reach the end of your rope, tie a knot in it and hang on."[5]

Part II

THE RESIDENTS: A COLLECTIVE STORY OF HOPE

- Four -

I'm Here to Help Grandpa

Our children's very future will be jeopardized if we don't begin creating and honoring more GrandFriendships…Now.[1]

—Helene Block Fields, *Don't Cheat the Children*

Once we finally had access to the housing and a small staff, it was less than two months before seniors and families began to move in. At that point, we were ready to accept referrals for children who had no place to call home. I will always be surprised—actually stunned—and deeply saddened every time I learn about the experiences of yet another child who has been in foster care. I will never get used to their stories—to what they and their birthparents, especially their mothers, have had to endure. Following are the stories that Marty and I put together of Marcus and Kenny, part of the first cohort of children to move to Hope Meadows.[2]

MARCUS

Like so many of the children who came to Hope, the first years of Marcus' and his sister Tasha's life were filled with violence, neglect, and loss. Marcus was born with drugs in his system. His mother, in her mid-twenties, had already lost parental rights to six previous children. Upon leaving the hospital, Marcus was placed with his paternal grandmother, but after two years she became ill and could no longer care for him. He went to live with his father and mother (who were cohabitating against court orders). Two months later there was an incident of domestic violence involving his mother and father, both of whom were intoxicated. His mother, eight months pregnant, ended up in the hospital, where she gave birth prematurely to Tasha, her ninth child. Tasha weighed less than five pounds.

Marcus remained with his father, living on the street during the day and sleeping in an abandoned house at night. When a charity offered money for a motel, Marcus' mother joined them once again, this time with Tasha. After only four days they were evicted and moved into a shelter. Soon a home health nurse checking on the baby found her parents had not kept any medical appointments. Tasha had not gained any weight, and she had diarrhea. There were no diapers, no formula, and no money to buy these things. At this point, the children were placed in a foster home where it is believed they were sexually abused.

Within six months, the children's mother died of an ectopic pregnancy. Eighteen months after that, their father's parental rights were terminated. Two years later, both children moved to Hope Meadows. Marcus was eight and Tasha was four.

Marcus was quiet when he first arrived; he didn't trust anyone and was described as joyless. He exhibited signs of anger and depression, had trouble sleeping, and didn't know how to play.

Sue, his Hope mom, said he would destroy any toy he was given. He hoarded food, wet his bed, and became defiant at bath time. At age eight, he did not know his ABCs and could not count or write his name.

After three years of life at Hope Meadows with Tasha and his adopted family, Marcus excelled in cross-country, T-ball, drawing, and scouts. No longer isolated or friendless, he and a band of Hope girls and boys regularly rode bikes around the neighborhood to check on the older adults they had not seen for a day or two. One of those seniors was Eileen Cromlich.

Eileen had shattered her arm in a fall down some steps. With surgery she was given a new plastic shoulder and a titanium arm shank. When she returned home, her daughters came to help her. She was in a great deal of pain and would spend her days and nights on her couch. Eileen told this story to a reporter:

> Every day Marcus would come to visit, and he'd stand with the other kids and never say anything. Then one day he said, 'Mrs. C, do you have to spend the rest of your life on that couch?'
>
> I smiled. 'No, I'll get up and be about.'
>
> 'Oh,' he asked, 'When?'
>
> 'Whenever I can,' I promised. Later, I told my girls, 'If anyone sees Marcus coming, you get me up and sitting on a chair!' Well. The next day, here he came, and they got me up. When Marcus saw me, he just grinned from ear to ear. You know, I'm up and about now because of these kids.[3]

Marcus grew close to several other seniors. Grandpa Harry, retired from the news business, taught him how to play croquet and took him to swim lessons in the summer. When Harry vacationed in Florida one winter, he called Marcus regularly—just to see how he was doing. Another senior, Esther Buttitta, began tutoring Marcus soon after his arrival. One day she told me with surprise that he'd actually laughed during their meeting and "had a twinkle in his eye!" And then there were Helen and Pat Hall, two *grandfriends* who were consistently involved in Marcus' life. When Pat was hospitalized on several occasions, Marcus was sure to make him a get-well card. Back home in Hope, Pat often could be seen riding his motorized wheelchair at full speed up and down the sidewalks of the neighborhood, with a smiling Marcus sitting on his lap.

In three years, Marcus grew from an introverted, sad little boy into a happy eleven-year-old with a warm demeanor. Esther was right—he most certainly had developed a twinkle in his eye and deep and dependable relationships with friends, grandmas and grandpas. Embraced by his Hope family, he learned to both give and receive love. We could all see this transformation, including the afterschool coordinator at Hope, who reported what might seem like—but was not—an ordinary exchange between mother and child:

> Yesterday, Sue Brown came to pick up her kids from the community center and stopped to talk with the seniors. As she was talking, I heard a child's voice say, 'Mom… Mommm.'
>
> Sue answered, 'Yeeesss?'
>
> 'I love you,' the child said, shyly…tentatively.
>
> I turned and looked to see it was Marcus…holding his new mom tightly as she said, 'I love you, too, Marcus. I love you too![4]

KENNY

Kenny, another cute but troubled young boy, was born the third of nine children. He was first placed in foster care due to neglect when he was just a year old. Over the next four years, Kenny was shuttled back and forth between his parents' home and a total of six foster homes. During this time, his mother—diagnosed with multiple forms of mental illness and living with an abusive drug dealer—had four more children. In this large and complex family, Kenny was ignored and left to fend for himself.

When he came to Hope Meadows at age five, what I remember most was that Kenny had no sense of self. He could not use a personal pronoun like "I" or "mine." When asked to draw pictures of his family, he drew stick figures of his birth parents and his siblings, but when adding himself to the picture he drew only a body, arms and legs—with no head. Besides severe neglect, Kenny had endured physical abuse, including being burned by cigarettes and (according to his own account) being thrown into deep water by his father where he almost drowned for lack of knowing how to swim.

Kenny's first few years at Hope were difficult. Frequent temper tantrums led to his placement in a special class in school for children with behavior disorders and he regularly ran away from home and school. Grandpa Al lived next door. Whenever Kenny disappeared it seemed that Al always knew where to find him, how to talk to him to find out what was the matter, and get him back home. They became the best of friends.

It was two years before Kenny's birthparents had their parental rights terminated. Finally, he could be adopted. We held an adoption party for him and later that day when we asked him what adoption meant to him he said, "DCFS is no longer the boss of me. I can stay with my mom forever and ever and ever. Now

I can go way out of our state. I have two sisters and one brother. I am glad they are my brother and sisters. They are adopted too, just like me."[5]

Kenny had always struggled with reading. When he started sixth grade, Hope senior Mary Ann Daly offered to tutor him. They met every Thursday afternoon to work on homework and cram for tests. Mary Ann told us this:

> It was a challenge to get everything finished because he really didn't understand much of what had been discussed in school, making re-teaching necessary before we could begin memorizing facts for a test. Getting his thoughts on paper was nearly impossible unless we worked together, sentence by sentence. He did work hard, however, always willing to try a new technique, or do something over. When all else failed he might just dig down to the bottom of his backpack, and clean some items out of it! We had an interesting year, but I didn't see a lot of progress.
>
> Seventh grade was a different story, due mostly to his resource room teacher, who posted homework daily on the internet, and always answered questions posed by parents and tutors. Kenny bloomed, was passing everything, and suddenly he could read a social studies question at the end of a lesson, flip pages, and point to the paragraph with the answer. There was suddenly some sort of inner locus of—if not control—success, ability…something that made him decide that schoolwork was not only doable but should be done to the best of his ability.
>
> When faced with a reading course second semester, we hit on a plan I call 'Feed Him and Read.' In addition to the usual Thursday homework sessions, Kenny would

> arrive on Saturdays as soon as his morning paper route was completed, and I'd feed him an enormous breakfast. Then we'd sit down and read, not the usual high interest/low vocabulary stuff, but all sorts of science fiction, which he'd chosen from a teacher-approved list. Now Kenny doesn't need my help with much of the reading, but our breakfast sessions continue, and will—just as long as he chooses to come. Tutoring Kenny has been a joy! Watching him develop as a reader, watching his self-confidence soar as his abilities improve, makes me very glad I'm here at Hope, using my professional training in retirement, and not totally put out to pasture.[6]

Fast forward to Kenny's senior year in high school. Mary Ann had done her job well and Kenny had become an avid reader. He and Grandpa Al stayed close. As Al's health declined, and especially after the Alzheimer's diagnosis, Kenny was the one to come by after school and read aloud to him. Al loved to see his Hope grandson and loved reminding me, "I'm here to help Kenny," something he had been saying and doing for years.

Funny thing: if you asked Kenny, he would always say, "I'm here to help Grandpa Al."

Who was helping whom?

FOR BIRTH MOTHERS, A LIFE OF DESPAIR

A few years after Hope Meadows was established, we compiled an aggregate profile of the children's birthmothers. The average birth mom had 4.7 children in partnership with 3.4 birth fathers. Twenty-nine percent of the mothers were raised in single parent households; fourteen percent allegedly were abused as children; and nearly one in four allegedly were sexually abused as a child, adult or both. One in ten became a mother while still a teenager. Almost half had a criminal record, and seventy-one percent were known to abuse drugs and alcohol, yet less than half had ever been involved in drug or alcohol treatment programs. Thirty-eight percent were diagnosed with a mental health problem, and an equal number had a history of unstable living situations. Not much could be confirmed about the birth fathers, but records indicated that most—sixty-five percent—were never involved in their children's lives.

These parent profiles helped to put into context the emotional and behavioral problems so many of the children had, and it explained why it was so difficult for the parents to get their children returned to them. But getting to know birthparents added an entirely new dimension to these understandings. One mother I came to know was sexually assaulted four times before she turned fourteen. Mary had a long history of severe mental illness and gave birth to ten children by six different fathers. While she had no record of drug or alcohol abuse, by the time three of her kids had come to Hope Meadows she was living with a man who used and sold drugs and who, it was alleged, had sexually abused one or more of her children. For those of us who have not even come close to experiencing such trauma, it is almost impossible to imagine Mary's past and present life.

In getting to know Mary and other birth mothers, I came to understand that with very few exceptions, they loved their children. Their incapacity to provide a safe environment, and the nurture and intellectual building blocks that all children need only added to the pain, turmoil, and chaos these women experienced in their daily lives. Like their children, they desperately needed to be surrounded by people who could support them and who cared deeply about them.

SELECTING THE CHILDREN—PAINFUL CHOICES

When children like Kenny and Marcus were referred to Hope, we weren't always given many details about their circumstances or the families from whom they were separated. But we knew their lives had been filled with emotional pain, fear, and uncertainty, much of which was due to neglect. We knew that often their parents were simply not there to protect them or to let them know they were loved. We knew many were hungry, living without toys or books or even beds to sleep in. We knew most had experienced the terror of environmental violence—dads beating up moms and shootings in the street—and multiple moves within the foster care system. The details were always variations on these themes. Our state agencies were overrun with children suffering in these ways. We heard rumors of kids sleeping in the offices of well-meaning case managers for lack of an appropriate foster home placement.

It helped us to help the children when we knew something about their birth parents, but sometimes nothing was known. One infant referred to us from Chicago had been found—hours old—abandoned in a hospital restroom. Wrongly diagnosed as a "drug baby," he was placed on a respiration monitor, and the search for a home began. No one wanted him—an infant with an unknown background and suspect health. Out of options, the state placed him in a privately-run institution, where he remained for three-and-a-half months until DCFS, citing the "mounting costs of private care," moved him again, this time into emergency foster care. Finally—after eighteen calls—the caseworker found us.

Referrals never stopped—more than we could ever place in the homes of the twelve to fifteen adoptive families living in

Hope at any given time. In the first six months of 1996 we were asked to find homes for forty-four kids—numbers well over our families' total capacity to care. Of these, five were sibling groups of kids ranging in age from one to seven. One was a sibling group of four and two were sibling groups of three. Always the children already in our homes and their needs came first, so rarely after Hope was a year old were placement of such large sibling groups viable. On one occasion, we received a referral for a sibling group of four boys, the oldest thirteen. Their father had died from a drug overdose and their mother from AIDS. That same day, when the *Nightline* crew showed up unexpectedly to continue filming, I shared the painful choice we had to make with their reporter, along with my personal regret: "We want to take *all* of these children…and we simply can't." It was a sad reality.

Space wasn't the only issue. We were often asked to provide homes for boys ages eight and older with histories of severe aggression or sexual abuse and who may have abused other children. Again, we did what we could to determine if there were Hope families who could provide a safe and supportive environment for these children and keep other children in the family safe as well. It was complicated from the start.

Families with even the slightest chance of being a good fit were contacted and given the information we had. Commonly, most of them reached out to other families in the community and to our Hope family advocate before making a decision to receive a child into their home. The choice was theirs in the end.

Our parents were both wise and realistic when deciding whether a child might fit well into their rapidly expanding family, but they never shied away from accepting some very troubled kids who they knew were coming in with tremendous baggage—*kids no one else wanted.* They knew they had the support of other families and the seniors, and with counseling and therapy only a doorstep away, they were willing and eager to give these kids a chance. On top of the trauma they experienced in the foster care system, all of the children in Hope had one or more of the following characteristics: a history of drug exposure; medical or physical conditions such as seizures, cerebral palsy, failure to thrive, diabetes, asthma, severe vision and hearing impairment; emotional and behavioral problems such as hyperactivity, impulsivity, enuresis, and trust, attachment, and loss issues; developmental and/or intellectual disabilities; and always a history of abuse (sexual, physical, emotional).

In our initial assessments of every child, we worked to identify both strengths and needs in order to plan an array of services that would support the child and all other family members. The goal was to help our children integrate their past into the present so that they could learn new coping skills, develop a sense of trust and safety, and ultimately form attachments—caring relationships—with their new families and neighbors. We wanted them to have a happy childhood, something they had never known before coming to Hope.

"Relationships," the late Peter Benson once said, "are the oxygen of human development. All young people need and deserve many adults who connect—and connect deeply with them."[7] The multiple warm and caring relationships Marcus, Kenny, and all of the kids at Hope Meadows had with their adopted families and grandparents were the oxygen they desperately needed to grow, learn, and become caring adults and productive citizens.

- Five -

The Parents: A Giant Leap of Faith

> When I read or hear about the happy experiences of adoptive families, I get that warm "goosepimply" feeling. Words like great, wonderful, fantastic, superb dance through my mind. Then I begin to wonder about those glowing reports. Are these people real? Does anyone else but me have problems and heartaches because of adoption?[1]
>
> —Donna Holmes, adoptive parent

Our adoptive parents were the true heroes of Hope Meadows, determined, loving and enduring all things. They were a diverse group. Six years after Hope's founding, approximately half were black and half were white. A majority were married, all had a high school education, approximately a third had some college, and another third had one or more college degrees.

With these differences, they still had much in common. All moved to Hope to complete their families or to start new families through adoption, and they viewed the arrival of a child as a precious gift. Like most parents, they believed the ultimate responsibility for strong families—those that are child-centered and emotionally bound with love—resides with the parents themselves. But these parents possessed a special wisdom and foresight most families do not have: they understood the road ahead would be complicated for them and for the very special children coming to them from the foster care system. Knowing they would need a community of caring people around them, embracing and supporting their families, they chose Hope.

In adoptive families of children who've experienced deep and pervasive trauma, successful parenting is especially hard work emotionally, physically, and intellectually. As Marty and I found out through our adoption studies in the 1980s, these children bring wounds and burdens with them into their adoptive homes, and the expression of those troubles impact their ability to integrate into family life. For parents, this almost inevitable set of circumstances leads to self-doubt and disillusionment and it can finally lead to isolation, if adoptive families find no one—professional or lay—who can understand what they experience and help them. Hope parents were no different in the beginning. Like the Sheppards and the Johnsons, they too questioned their decision to adopt at times, and their ability to be "good" parents. But Hope families had somewhere to turn—their neighbors, the seniors who moved there to support their families, and the other adoptive families who did understand, could listen, care, and lend a hand. To orchestrate and guide this community support, the Hope staff was always there to help.

PARENT SUPPORT

We organized to give Hope parents as much support as possible. Once a month, parents participated in family team meetings.

These meetings provided a forum for improved communication and problem-solving, where parents could share concerns and successes, and could work together with staff to ensure that the varying and individual needs of their children would be addressed within the family and community. Our *Parent Advisory Committee* gave them the opportunity to help refine the support structure for future adoptive parents.

What many found most helpful was the daily contact they had with each other and the one-on-one contact they had—sometimes daily and almost always in their homes—with Hope's family advocate. This advocate, who was a champion listener and empathetic, was indispensable in helping parents learn to create a shared, successful adoption story within the context of an intimate community that often felt a bit like a fish bowl—or a very small town. This was never easy for any of the parents, but they were committed to their children and to what the experiment of Hope Meadows was trying to accomplish. Two moms, Elsa and Beverly, had very different experiences; both were eloquent in sharing their stories.

ELSA

Elsa Raab, a research analyst with two master's degrees—one in computer science and another in library information and science—lived in a condo in Chicago before moving to Hope Meadows. "There," she confessed, "I didn't even know my neighbors' names. I'd ride up the elevator with them and we didn't speak. It is so incredibly different here. I do feel like I'm part of a community now."[2]

Already the single parent of one adopted child when she moved to Hope, Elsa eventually adopted three more children, none of whom was biologically related to another, and each of a different race. She wrote the following essay which creatively and realistically describes life as an adoptive parent in this special community.

The Adoption Symphony

When I think about adoption, I am reminded of a symphony. The conductor raises his baton, and each individual blends his own music into the orchestra's triumphal and glorious rendition. The composer's talent, as well as each orchestra member's musicianship, is enhanced by being a part of the whole. The symphony's success hinges on the music of each player individually. The evening's performance, however, does not come without a price. Thousands of hours of individual practice, group practice, musical experience, and the composer's own travail in birthing the symphony have preceded the beautiful music. Mistakes, wrong notes, re-writing, practice, and more practice have been a part of the final product.

Our journey as an adoptive family during the last few years has been much like an orchestra preparing a symphony. As the conductor and composer of this symphony, I am thrilled when we hit the right notes, when all of our practice comes together, when each member is playing his part, and the music is truly heaven-sent. These times are the confirming moments when I realize how blessed our family has been by adoption. The musical moments come at strange times—tucking a child into bed at night, a family discussion in the van in route to school, enjoying a basketball game together, or the many hugs and kisses and 'I love you[s]' that never seem to end.

However, the music of adoption is not always so beautiful. As our symphony is just now being written, we sometimes need to go back and re-write a measure. Figuring out the notes of the music sometimes takes a lot of trial and error. As we learn to be a family, each one of us has brought different backgrounds and different traumas to the music. Many times, we play sour notes. But as we practice and learn individually, and as we come together to practice and learn together as a family, the quality of our music improves.

We are trying to put very different instruments together to make a beautiful sound. The flute is very different from the drum, and the saxophone and viola add even more sounds. When each player tries to play on his own without blending with the other instruments, dissonance results! We need to learn to play together. Each instrument has its own unique place in our orchestra. Working together as a family has taken hours and hours (and weeks and months and years) of practice. And, quite often, the conductor herself learns and grows from the instrumentalists, and realizes that she needs to make some changes in how she conducts!

Although our symphony journey is filled with practices and work and sour notes and long hours and working together despite all odds, when I hear the beautiful music of our family in its full harmony, I know that I have been blessed to travel this journey. And I know that God orchestrated this symphony in placing Kate, Jerome, Greg, Maria and Elsa as the major players for the music.

Six years ago, I didn't have my orchestra. I lived a fairly normal life in a fairly normal world. I didn't have to spend hours and hours practicing, work at blending together various instruments who each wanted to play their own sour notes, compose a major symphony, and put my life into creating a cohesive unit from five very different members.

But I also didn't have the music.[3]

When human experience is complex, we need metaphor to adequately describe it. For Elsa, life in an adoptive family is a symphony. For the late Urie Bronfenbrenner, a renowned professor of human development at Cornell University, raising children is like an especially lively game of table tennis. He concludes that the intellectual, emotional, social, and moral development of children requires, "high levels of motivation, attentiveness, sensitivity, and persistence on the part of both participants." This, he summarizes, occurs "…in the context of an escalating ping-pong game between two people who are crazy about each other."[4] Both metaphors tell the truth: for adoptive families, strong, mutual attachment—an unfolding development of children and healthy family life—does not happen instantaneously.

I think it would be hard to imagine the commitment it takes to weather the ups and downs of parenting without being one. Maria Shriver said, "Having kids—is the biggest job anyone can embark on. As with any risk, you have to take a leap of faith and ask lots of wonderful people for their help and guidance."[5] For all the parents, and particularly for Beverly Connor, the risk was monumental and would have been unimaginable without the support of the Hope community.

BEVERLY

Beverly Connor and her husband Larry were a middle-aged couple active in the community and well-liked by everyone. The children were especially drawn to Larry. He had spent part of his youth in the system, and he knew he could help other children who had been uprooted like he had been. He understood their pain, confusion, and insecurity. As Bev once said, "His caring came through."

It wasn't long after moving to Hope before they became pre-adoptive foster parents to four children; two were siblings who had lived in ten different foster homes. The children's ages ranged from nine years to four months old. With Bev and Larry, they'd finally found a family where they were safe, cared for, and loved. Cassie, the oldest child, once wrote me a letter thanking me for helping them all to find "the best home ever."

> Dear Brenda,
>
> These are the reasons I like being in Bev and Larry's house. First of all, they take us out to Sirloin Stockade. And they care for us. They are the best mom and dad in the entire universe. They take the time to talk to me about my feelings. Nobody ever took the time for that. They let us go on long rides, walks, picnics, hikes, and trips. This is the best home I ever been in.[6]

One night, after the children had been with the Connors for about two years, Bev woke up at 2 a.m. to find Larry struggling to breathe and in pain. She first called 911 and then senior neighbors Loralee and her husband, Al, who had served as a medic in the military. An ambulance soon arrived and took Larry to the hospital—he was having a heart attack. Bev followed with another Hope parent who had heard the sirens and had come running down the street to see if she could help her close friend. Marty and I pieced together what happened next.

Al and Loralee spent the night with the children in the Connor's home. The next morning, they had the very sad task of delivering the news which no one had expected: their beloved Larry had died. The couple comforted the children, answered their questions, and assured them that it was going to be okay. They cleaned the house and made meals, giving Bev time and space to absorb this sudden tragedy. Larry was only fifty-one. Loralee told us about that night:

> Little Matthew heard everything, absolutely word for word—everything [while Bev, Al, and the medics were attending to Larry]. He wanted to tell the girls what he heard and what he knew happened in the night. Cassie was mad…and asked, 'Why did he have to die?'
>
> I just talked with them. They were all concerned about whether they would be allowed to stay. Would Bev be able to keep them? 'I can't answer that,' I said, 'but I know that she wants to. She'll love you forever,' I added, 'and we will always be your grandma and grandpa. We'll always love you…' I just talked with them like this for a long time.

As word spread about Larry's death, neighbors came to help. One senior, John, remembered events with tears in his eyes:

> We knew Bev would be at the hospital most of the day and she wouldn't have time...so a bunch of us seniors just pitched in. We straightened up the house from the night before…cleaned up the kitchen. Al cleaned up the bedroom. He picked up the bandages and needles and stuff that the paramedics had left there from the night before.

Two days later, neighbors and staff held a special visitation for all the children living at Hope Meadows, including Bev's kids. Bev described it like this:

> It was amazing how everybody at the visitation worked with the kids and let them go around doing what they wanted to do. They talked to each other and they cried and several of them touched Larry and made pictures for him and my kids wrote him letters, and they put them under his coat. There was not a lot of commotion or anything. Children were crying softly. They would come up and talk to me. They were worried about me, and I was worried about them. It was wonderful.

Larry was buried on the day he and Bev were to adopt their first child. Through these extremely difficult days, Bev was brave, strong, and courageous. As a now-single parent, with the entire community to support her, she would go on to adopt three of the four children she and Larry had taken into their home. Like all parents she had her ups and downs in raising these children:

> Sometimes I get very tired and sometimes the kids get very tired and I wonder if I can make it... But, with the support of the grandparents, the counselors, and the Hope families, I believe I can. Some call me all the time and some of them I don't see that much. Some check and make sure I'm okay and if I need anything. If I get sick they are there asking if I want somebody to watch the kids. I was real sick last week, and so was Matthew. People called to run errands—they got our prescriptions. They cooked dinner and brought it over.

> They took my kids after school so I could rest. They were marvelous.[7]

Larry's death was especially difficult for Matthew. Just when he was beginning to feel safe, the loss of a new father who loved and cared for him became an insurmountable crisis, an "adverse childhood experience."[8] It seemed to be a turning point for Matthew, a moment past which he could no longer allow himself to trust others, to care about others, or to allow others to care about him. A year after Larry died, Bev decided she could no longer provide the intensive parenting Matthew needed and be a good parent to her other three children. Because no other families at Hope were possible fits for him, DCFS reluctantly moved Matthew to the home of a biological relative who lived in a nearby town. He was never adopted.

NANCY

Like Bev, Nancy also needed more help than the Hope community could provide to meet the needs of a child she came to care deeply about. Tragically this off-site professional help was not provided.

Nancy was single, herself adopted, and forty-six when she moved to Hope. She loved the idea of community support, the many opportunities to participate in community activities, and the real possibility of parenting an older child. When she first met Dwayne, she immediately fell under his spell. This was the child she had been longing for.

Nine-year-old Dwayne was cute, intelligent, and extremely charismatic, but we soon learned he also was highly troubled and angry. From birth he had endured harsh and aggressive treatment, the ongoing incarceration of his parents, abandonment by his father, and a life of severe poverty lived in sometimes squalid conditions.

Eighteen months after coming to us, Dwayne's anger was unabated, and he began to exhibit exceptionally troubling behaviors. Within a two-week period, Nancy and I repeatedly called for help from doctors and service providers, hoping a change in medication might make a difference. On one of those days, several encounters with Dwayne left Nancy afraid for her safety. Paramedics transported the boy to a local hospital twenty minutes away; I followed the ambulance and begged to have him admitted for a medical evaluation. Without it we could not guarantee safety for either Nancy or for Dwayne. Despite my pleas, he was not admitted. Instead, he was removed from our community, disappearing back into the revolving door of the foster care system.

Nancy, I, and others in the community had become very attached to Dwayne. Five years after he was taken away from Hope, we conducted a survey of our seniors in which we asked them to name one of their biggest disappointments since coming to Hope. To our surprise, a number of them said it was that they were not able to do enough to help Dwayne.

Over the years Nancy and I kept track of Dwayne. By age sixteen, he'd moved seventeen times, shuffled back and forth between foster homes, institutions, and his birthmother's home. At age seventeen, he was charged with a double murder. Because he was a minor, he was "ineligible" for the death penalty, but if found guilty, under Illinois law he would spend the remainder of his life behind bars with no chance for parole. It would take two more trials (first a mistrial and then a hung jury) and nearly three more years in jail before this young man would be found by a jury to be innocent of all charges. Although these trials were extremely difficult to sit through, both Nancy and I attended all three. We were not allowed to speak with Dwayne, not one word, but our presence let him know we still cared and had never forgotten him. Nancy gave up on her dream to parent a child, but she remained at Hope for many years, playing scrabble in the evenings with neighbors and helping out wherever and whenever she could. We have both stayed in touch with Dwayne, who is now thirty years old.

Dwayne continues to struggle with relationships and maintaining employment due primarily to problems with anger management. In his twenties and in jail for a relatively minor infraction, he once wrote to me and asked, "How can I believe in myself when no one else believes in me?"[9] He'd recently contacted his mother from jail and asked her to pick up a paycheck from his last job. His mother agreed, cashed the check, and spent every penny on herself. Is it any wonder that Dwayne is unable to believe anyone truly cares about him?

Bev and Nancy weren't perfect parents. No one is. But they were both committed to the work and the people of Hope. Despite loss and failure, Bev endured as a committed, adoptive parent to her children, and Nancy became a strong support to everyone in our community. But adoptive parenting was not for everyone. For some the challenges were too great, even with daily support, and a handful of parents turned out not to be a good fit for Hope Meadows. In two cases, single parents married after coming to Hope, and their new spouses did not want to build a family through adoption. Another couple adopted a child whom they deeply cared about, but the father could not commit to adopting again, and for career reasons he wanted to move to a more affluent and bigger community. Two couples, both veteran foster parents, could not adjust to the Hope ethos. They knew the foster care system and its requirements, and they could run efficient foster care homes, but neither chose to accept and commit to our Hope vision, including the full integration of Hope children into their home and family.

The majority of Hope parents came to accept, appreciate, and rely on the community for support. The children they embraced were some of the most troubled in the Illinois foster care system. To a person, these parents tell us they could never have gotten to the point of adoption without the support and understanding of one another, the seniors, and our staff. "No way," one mom told me, "could I have survived on my own without all this support."

Knowing how important they would be in the lives of these children and how challenging their jobs would be, our Hope parents took a giant leap of faith. They uprooted their lives, and in some cases, sacrificed careers and dreams to become adoptive parents and live in a community where they would both give and receive help and guidance for the sake of their families. They certainly didn't see themselves as heroes, but rather as ordinary people living extraordinary lives in a truly extraordinary community.

- Six -

It's Really a Wonderful Life

> Lacking a coherent view of how people might live successfully all the way to their very end, we have allowed our fates to be controlled by the imperatives of medicine, technology, and strangers.[1]
>
> —Atul Gawande, *Being Mortal*

If the parents were the true heroes of Hope Meadows, the seniors were its bedrock. While a fraction of the seniors did not find Hope a good fit and left, most who moved there, enveloped in a culture of neighborliness and care, benefited as much as the children and parents. Many lived there "successfully all the way to their very end," as illustrated by the following stories about George, Esther, and Steve.

GEORGE KING

George and his wife Effie were the first seniors to move to Hope Meadows. Effie was born in a tiny town in Mississippi, the sixth of twelve children. She moved to Illinois at the age of fifteen. George, one of nine siblings, was also born in Mississippi but moved to Illinois when he was very young. Their moves from Mississippi to Illinois were a part of the great migration of African Americans during the early-to-middle part of the 20th Century. George and Effie were married when she was twenty-one and he was thirty-one. Neither had graduated from high school. Together they raised seven biological children, two nephews, and numerous foster children prior to their arrival at Hope. George served in the Army for six years. After leaving the military he had various jobs, including employment as a factory worker, cook, and a bus driver. Eventually, unable to work because of a heart condition, he went on SSI disability. At the time he and Effie moved to Hope Meadows, George required the assistance of a home health nurse. Later we were told that doctors had predicted he would live no more than two years past that time. He definitely proved them wrong!

George began volunteering as a crossing guard three blocks from his house at the edge of Hope Meadow's property, starting at 7:30 in the morning. He described his routine in this way:

> I'd leave there [his crossing guard position] about 9:00, and I'd come back home and go at 9:30 to the playground, and I'd leave the playground and go to the community center about 11:00. I'd come back home, have a cup of coffee and then go back to the crossing guard. Then after the kids were home, I'd go back to the community center until 5:30.

After living at Hope Meadows for three months, George told his home health nurse not to come back, "…cuz you interfere with my time. I've got things I have to do." He surely did.

George was out and about every day. He loved being a part of the Hope community. I remember once going into our community center in the late afternoon. George was on the carpeted floor with two children crawling over him. What joy was on his face! Dressed in a shirt, tie, slacks, and suspenders, he often could be found playing checkers with the kids or watching them at the playground. After they had lived at Hope Meadows for over a year, Effie described his transformation: "I've watched this man. I've watched the healing in him. It wasn't all sickness. It was loneliness. I've watched this man come alive. I mean, I watch him have a reason to get up in the morning, and when night comes, he is so tired."

Fourteen years after moving to Hope Meadows and throughout the last year of his life, George—at seventy-nine—was still engaged in the community, getting around on a motorized wheelchair equipped with oxygen cylinder and cannula, attending events, debating issues with neighbors, and eloquently advocating for the children and our intergenerational way of life whenever opportunities arose. He would always say, "We are making history." What I will remember most about George was his humility, his perpetual smile, and his warm, infectious laughter permeating the neighborhood. Effie told me recently, "In our nearly fifty years of marriage, I never saw George as happy as he was here at Hope."

REMEMBERING ESTHER

Several years ago, Marty and I worked with Esther Buttitta to put together the following story. Like many at Hope Meadows, Esther was a special person. She found a way to give and receive, to care and be cared for, to find purpose, meaning, and joy in each day. Here is her story—a tribute to one fine lady.

Esther was born in 1927, the youngest of three children. Her father was a civil engineer for the United States government. His job required moving often from project to project, primarily within the Midwest. Upon graduation from high school, she entered college on a four-year scholarship. Her mother died just after her sophomore year, and Esther had to leave college to help care for her father. She married John when she was twenty. Soon followed five children.

John hurt his back and went on partial SSI disability when Esther was in her mid-thirties. Esther returned to school for a degree in teaching. As the new family breadwinner, she began her teaching career at age thirty-six in a six-room schoolhouse on the edge of a small Central Illinois town, where she continued to work even after the birth of two more children. John, Esther, and all seven of their children volunteered often in this small town, helping neighbors and through their church. Esther said this: "The Lord put us on this Earth to spread His bounty, and you are supposed to use your talents, not hide them. We felt the more we did for others, the more we would get in return, and that is how John and I lived, and our children did too."

As she approached sixty, Esther looked forward to retirement with her husband. But John died suddenly in an automobile accident, and for the next ten years she struggled to recover her life. She lived in several places, but nothing seemed to work for her. During these difficult years, Esther's health deteriorated. She underwent two hip replacement surgeries, back surgery, and a heart bypass operation. While recuperating from heart surgery, she came across an article about Hope Meadows. Seventy years old and in poor health, Esther still believed she had much to contribute to this unique community. She did just that for years—participating in our preschool program, tutoring school-age children, and helping with arts and crafts, quilting, and sewing.

Esther described life in Hope this way:

> You wake up in the morning and you hurt, you know. And you go out and meet someone and you're busy with the children, and you forget about how bad you feel. It raises your spirits...it keeps you young. I feel important when I'm around the children. *It's really a wonderful life!*

After living at Hope Meadows for a little more than two years, Esther began to experience debilitating back pain. She was recuperating after surgery in a rehabilitation facility when her doctors insisted she could never return to Hope Meadows—she needed far too much care. Esther replied, "You do not know Hope."

No, he did not. Several weeks after returning to us, she wrote the following letter for *Seedlings,* the weekly Hope Meadows newsletter:

> To all of you at Hope Meadows,
>
> Thank you for everything:
>
> For feeding me a hot meal each day.
>
> For transporting me by car, walker and wheelchair to the many appointments.
>
> For running errands, bringing in the mail and the newspaper.
>
> For inspiring me to improve. Your prayers are appreciated.
>
> For keeping me posted as to the happenings in our neighborhood.
>
> I do miss the personal contact with our kids.

> For being patient when I experience loss of memory from the medications.
>
> You make my world a better place.
>
> Thank you again and again.
>
> Sincerely, Esther Buttitta

Bill, Esther's next-door neighbor, spent sixteen years in the military and was wounded in action more than once. Before moving to Hope, he'd retired from seventeen years as a diesel mechanic. Bill liked to keep busy and when someone was sick, he was always there to help them out. During Esther's illness he drove her wherever she needed to go, including just across the street to a special event at Hope's community center. Several women in the neighborhood had put together an impromptu luncheon, and they called Bill to see if he could assist. Esther told this story:

> He helped me to the car and drove me across the street to have lunch with all the ladies. [After that] we started a new thing. I would say, 'Bill, I need someone to fix a meal for me.'
>
> And every time, Bill, who loved to cook, would ask, 'What do you want to eat?'
>
> And I'd tell him, 'Well, I thought I'd like—,' and then he'd check my freezer, get the food, fix it for me, and bring it over.

Bill, who was slightly younger than Esther, prepared a meal of her choice every day until she recovered. Just four months after her letter to the community, Esther was returning the favor—delivering food to another of her neighbors recently home from a hospital stay!

But Esther's health problems persisted. By the time she was seventy-seven she had arthritis, diabetes, a thyroid condition and heart failure. She needed oxygen from a tank to live, but she didn't give up. As it became increasingly difficult to get around, she spent less time at the community center doing her volunteer work and more time mentoring children in her home. She explained: "The children won't let me quit. They ring the doorbell and say, 'We're just checking on you today.' [When] they're here…you can't lie on the couch. You have to sit up and do things."

Marty, a Hope teenager Esther had tutored since he was four, visited her daily. She proudly told us that he visited regularly, "to just bring the paper or empty my trash; sometimes he brings me the mail. *I am his concern*. He's my boy! I'd do anything for that boy."

When we asked Marty why he spent so much time helping Esther, he simply replied, "because I love her."

Much of Esther's mentoring revolved around her interest in dolls. Her collection was extensive and she loved to make doll clothes, so the neighborhood children came to play with her dolls or bring their dolls to be outfitted with new clothes: "Peggy (age seven) will call me on the phone and ask, 'Grandma, are you lonesome?' And I'll say, 'Yeah,' and then she'll come in to play with the dolls. I've become known as the doll grandma."

Esther once told us about a visit she had from Tasha, Marcus' younger sister:

> The doorbell rang. Tasha came in asking if she could play with the dolls. After a while I asked her if she had a doll of her own.
>
> She shook her head and said no, so I told her that someone in [the Hope] office had given me the very doll she was

> playing with and that possibly it was meant for her. I wish I had a camera for that moment when she asked, 'For me?'
>
> 'Yes,' I said, 'Why don't you find her some clothes?' And so she did. We wrapped up the clothes, and I gave her a small tea set for the doll.
>
> When it was time for Tasha to go, I suggested that she put the doll in a sack, but she said, 'Oh, No!' Tasha wanted to carry that doll in her arms! Out she went to ride off on her bike. God love her!

Esther told us her greatest satisfaction was working with these children one-on-one, week- by-week, watching them develop physically and mentally. She mused, "I must have been chosen to show these children how to love. I love my job!" At Esther's funeral service a few years later, held in a small, rural (all white) Catholic church, sixteen-year-old (African American) Tasha courageously asked the parish priest if she could please sing a song before Mass began. He said no.

Tasha returned to her seat beside me, dejected. But somehow—perhaps persuaded by one of Esther's family—the priest changed his mind and allowed her to sing one of Esther's favorite hymns at the front of the church. She performed *acapella* with the voice of an angel, and we were all blessed.

STEVE DONAVAN

I knew that moving to Hope Meadows was life changing for many of the seniors. The relationships they formed with each other, the parents, and the children were often transformative, helping them to be their very best selves. But I remained in awe at how deeply important their daily experiences of giving and receiving care were to them. This was especially true for Steve Donavan.

Steve, the father of eight grown children, had retired from the military where he had held many administrative positions. He threw himself wholeheartedly into community activities during the time he lived at Hope Meadows. He loved to help mow lawns and the grassy areas of our common space. During his first summer at Hope he said, "Through mowing, I got to know just about everyone." At the end of that summer Steve had his first stroke. Over the next six years he would come to have three more, putting an end to his lawn-mowing and leading him instead to volunteer wherever and however he could. He was not a man to give up or give in to his medical issues.

His wife Kathy, quiet and not nearly as outgoing as Steve, often travelled out of state for her job. In her absence after his strokes the community pitched in to see to Steve's needs. Steve said, "Friends came out of the woodwork. Everyone brought food; they checked on me every day. "They took him out to lunch and helped to cut up his food if needed, drove him to rehabilitation therapy twice a week when Kathy wasn't home, and to Rotary meetings. He was always out and about. Because of the strokes, however, Steve's health continued to deteriorate. Knowing the end was near, he and Kathy left Hope Meadows to be near their children in another state.

At age seventy-five, Steve died. Kathy eventually moved back to Hope Meadows and as a licensed massage therapist, volunteered her services to the Hope residents. She set up a massage table in one of her spare bedrooms, but would often serve her neighbors in their homes at no charge. Kathy loved to remind us that Steve always described his ten years at Hope as the best years of his life. I couldn't believe it. "How can that be?" I asked her. "He had four strokes while he was here!"

"It was because he had so much to do, so many friends, and

so many people who cared about him. His life was full," she said softly, "and he felt truly blessed."[2]

TEN YEARS BEFORE THE BOOMERS

When Hope started in 1994, it would be over a decade before baby boomers would begin retiring at the rate of 10,000 a day, but even in 1994 vast numbers of older men and women, single or married, were unsatisfied with their lives and searching for something meaningful to do. Like Elmer and Margie, they came to Hope Meadows to find purpose, to make a difference in the lives of the children and their parents in our community.

Like George and Effie, most of the older and retired adults who first came to Hope lived within a thirty-mile radius of Rantoul. They heard about our program from local newspaper articles or word-of-mouth. But it wasn't long before seniors began to apply from all over the country, thanks to so much attention from national media.

Seniors interested in living at Hope were interviewed by both staff and residents. The requirements were minimal—they needed to pass a background check, pay a very affordable monthly rent, and convince us of their real interest in being a part of an active intergenerational community. We did keep an eye out for younger seniors who would, we assumed, be more active and present in the lives of the children for many years. While some self-selected out during that process, few were turned away.

Within two years all of our senior apartments were full. Approximately half of the seniors were single and half were married; half of the households had a senior who was employed; and over ninety percent were under seventy-five years of age. Just under seventy percent were white, and roughly one in five had a college education.[3] By the time we celebrated our tenth anniversary, just twenty percent of the senior households included an employed resident, reflecting a stable and aging population. But as our numbers grew, so did our percentage of seniors with a college education—rising from twenty to thirty-four percent over that same period.[4]

LIVING A LIFE THAT MATTERS

Life at Hope Meadows was rich and satisfying for most of our seniors, regardless of their education, background, income, and especially, regardless of their health. There were three key reasons for this.

First, like all other residents, they were *accepted for who they were*. While many had health issues (like nearly all of us once we reach a certain age), their neighbors—children, parents, and contemporaries—did not let health or mobility issues define them. A reciprocity of caring at Hope led easily to an acceptance of the physical and emotional realities of aging, based on the accepted certainty that our seniors contributed as friends, mentors, and surrogate grandparents to the betterment of our community. Health issues were considered circumstances to be addressed through accommodation or alteration, as with George in his wheelchair advocating for Hope, or Esther tutoring in her home when she couldn't make it to the community center. And when our seniors needed help, it was our purpose and our honor to step in, so that they were always supported and included as much as possible.

Second, the intentional neighboring model developed at Hope Meadows provided our *seniors with a clear and tangible purpose*. Before coming to Hope, so many of them, like Elmer, George, and Esther, felt bored, lonely, and a little useless. Having new purpose gave their lives meaning; they were needed—no longer dispensable. As a result, they found joy and acquired a renewed sense of self. Sherwin Nuland, in "The Art of Aging," writes, "We serve, we are indispensable, we have value in another's eyes and therefore in our own. The sense of being needed is the sense of purpose we all must find if life is to keep its meaning."[5]

Third, the seniors at Hope could see that *their ages, their histories and their accumulated experiences were highly valued assets* as they engaged in service to the community. Marc Freedman, a proven effective advocate for seniors, sent me a passage from the Talmud, telling the story of a rabbi passing thorough a field, and noticing an old man planting an acorn.

> 'Why are you planting that acorn?' the rabbi asks. 'You surely do not expect to live long enough to see it grow into an oak tree.'
>
> To which the old man—turning slowly from the ground to fix his glance on the not-so-wise clergyman—says, 'My ancestors planted seeds so that I might enjoy the shade and the fruit of trees. I do likewise for those who come after me.'

Marc went on to observe that "planting, tending, bequeathing to the next generation—it's the essential human project. For those of us who are old, our task is not to try to be young, but to be there for those who actually are."[6]

The seniors at Hope were engaged daily in this "essential human project." They did not—nor did their community—dwell on their age; they were living a life that mattered and in doing so, *they contributed.* As my colleague, Dr. David Racine, often said, "*Who they were*, not just what they did, mattered and had meaning."[7]

Hope Neighbors

photo credit: Judy Griesedieck

photo credit: Judy Griesedieck

photo credit: Carolyn Casteel

photo credit: Alex Harris, alex-harris.com/

photo credit: Judy Griesedieck

photo credit: Judy Griesedieck

photo credit: Caroline Greyshock

photo credit: Caroline Greyshock

photo credit: Bill Wiegand

photo credit: Alex Harris, alex-harris.com/

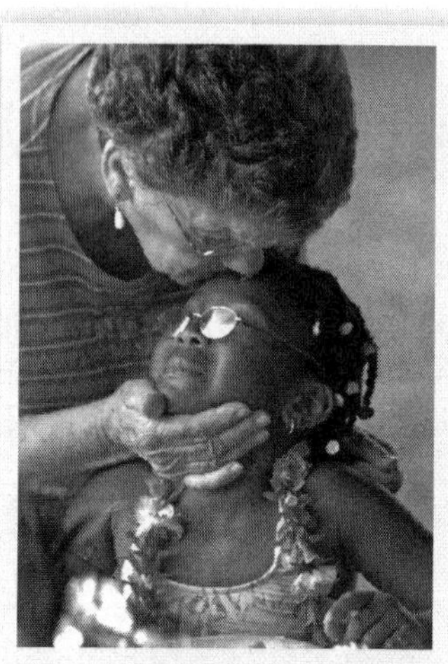

photo credit: Judy Griesedieck

photo credit: Alex Harris, alex-harris.com/

photo credit: Judy Griesedieck

photo credit: Caroline Greyshock

photo credit: Judy Griesedieck

photo credit: Alex Harris, alex-harris.com/

photo credit: Hope for the Children staff

photo credit: Caroline Greyshock

Part III

CORE VALUES, CORE INTENTIONS

- Seven -

Making the Big Difference: Caring Relationships

> Government can create economic and physical security and a just order, but meaning, joy and the good life flow from loving relationships, thick communities, and wise friends.[1]
>
> —David Brooks,
> Op-Ed for *The New York Times*

Being part of a caring community where a culture of neighborliness prevailed made it possible for George, Esther, Steve, Elsa, Beverly, and so many others to make a real difference in the lives of some very vulnerable children—and in the lives of one another. They could see their worth and purpose every day, and they knew they were a part of transforming the way children in foster care were loved and supported.

This Hope experience required all of our residents to cast aside three common and deeply-held beliefs—assumptions that place undue burdens on individuals and families and diminish the worth of people. The first is tied to our national value of independence and best described as the "bootstraps" theory of personal success. The second belief is an unhappy derivative of that theory, assuming those who can't always pull themselves up by their bootstraps—those who are vulnerable—are somehow "less-than" others, or problems to be solved, or burdens. The third assumption is that as we age our lives become less potent, our contributions less significant. At Hope we worked hard to transform these beliefs in favor of a collective and interdependent community response to human need, recognizing the value of every individual in our midst and the power of caring relationships among people of all ages.

This transformation was not automatic. How does one unlearn years of deep-rooted beliefs—values that guide us as we determine what is important in life? How do we change those guiding values that have directed our responses for so long, steered our decisions, and influenced the way we've lived alongside one another? *To see things differently and reject ingrained values takes time, new experiences, and a willingness to know ourselves and be mindful of our responses to others.* It is not easy. In my job as director at Hope Meadows, little that I did was more important than

- working with the Hope board, staff, and residents to align our mission and policies with values that represented new beliefs about the *power of caring relationships, vulnerability, and the significance of the lives of older adults; and,*
- helping staff and residents to become so conscious and deliberate in their daily interactions that over time implementation of our core values simply became routine, a taken-for-granted part of everyday life, and instrumental in shaping the culture of the community.

This and the next two chapters describe these three core values as they were lived out at Hope. They weren't our only values, but they were the ones that mattered most.

WE NEED ONE ANOTHER

Above all, we believed in *the power of caring relationships to foster wellbeing and the enduring capacity all of us have to form these relationships.* Embracing this value involves a critical shift in thinking about individuals and families, recognizing that neither individuals by themselves, nor any one family on its own, can overcome what seem to be insurmountable obstacles to wellbeing without the support and friendship of caring friends and neighbors. Ingrained in our culture is the belief that *family* can overcome just about anything as long as we can access treatment or services from appropriate professionals. We can work harder, love harder, try harder, and things will get better. We can pull ourselves up by our bootstraps and somehow emerge victorious. But the families in our original study of children in foster care, the birth families of the children who came to Hope Meadows from foster care, the adoptive families at Hope Meadows, and our seniors *all* needed more than their own personal strength and the expertise offered up by systems and institutions. For all of them, that was a recipe for isolation, powerlessness and ultimately hopelessness.

One key conclusion from Marty's and my initial study of pre-adoptive families in the 1980s reinforced this shift in our thinking: *Despite professional intervention, these families could not solve problems by themselves; they felt isolated and unsupported, with no one to talk to who understood firsthand the issues they were dealing with—no one with similar daily life experiences.* This truth was my primary impetus for starting Hope Meadows, and knowing it helped us to facilitate what parents at Hope Meadows loved most about our community: the daily contact they had with one another to share concerns, solve problems, and offer support. This contact was essential for the children and seniors as well. It was hard to tell what was more important to our residents: depending on others or caring for them.

Ultimately, Hope Meadows operated on this certainty: *children with special needs create families with special needs who, in turn, need a community of support*—a community of everyday people who believe in the importance of caring relationships for one's wellbeing to flourish, and who put this belief into daily action. For this to happen everyone needed both opportunities and encouragement. Our work at Hope, therefore, had to be deliberate and intentional, drawing into community those who needed relationships the most.

SOMETIMES IT TAKES TWO MOMS

Cathy and Jenny, both Hope parents, lived across the street from each other. Jenny's kids loved Cathy and thought of her as their aunt. Cathy described the relationship in a letter: "We spend time together daily and share meals together often. Jenny and I babysit for each other…we are very much like an extended family, as opposed to merely neighbors." She went on to tell this story:

> Jenny called me this morning and asked if I could come over to help calm Davie (age seven) down. He was being aggressive and making threatening statements. Jenny needed to get dressed, but she was afraid to leave Davie alone.
>
> When I arrived, Davie was sitting on a chair in the dining room. Jenny went upstairs and Davie and I began to talk. He was agitated and very angry. I asked him what was going on. He replied that he was mad because

> he didn't want to take his medicine. I asked him if he wanted to talk about what happened. He told me that when Jenny told him he needed to take it, he threw it, called her a "faggot," and told her to shut up. I asked him if he did anything else.
>
> "Yeah, I hit her."
>
> I asked him if he thought it was okay to hit someone when you are mad, and if he wanted to hurt his mom, himself, or others. His answers were always "Yes." After about twenty minutes, he let go of his anger and calmed down.

This was only one example of the way in which Jenny was able to draw help and support from her neighbor when she needed it. Cathy continued to write:

> There were two other times this week when Jenny called me to help calm Davie down. We've found that it helps if someone else is present. On Wednesday, he barricaded himself inside his bedroom closet. He was in a rage and wouldn't talk to Jenny, so I came over and talked to him through the closet doors. I asked him what was wrong. He said he didn't know how to do his math. I asked him if sitting in the closet was helping him learn how to do the math.
>
> "No," he admitted.
>
> "Would it be better to come out and get some help with it?"
>
> "I still won't know how to do it."
>
> "But I bet your mom will help you if you come out."
>
> Davie was silent.
>
> "Think about it, Davie," I said gently, "and come out when you're ready for some help." Ten minutes later he

> emerged from the closet, still not ready to do his math, but much calmer and willing to join the family.
>
> On Thursday night, Jenny called again and asked if I would come over because Davie refused to go to bed and was running wildly through the house. She thought the presence of another person would help Davie to calm down and go to bed. It worked. When Davie saw me, he stopped running and willingly went to bed. I stayed for about thirty minutes until he fell asleep and [then] helped Jenny get her other two kids into bed.[2]

As Cathy related these stories, she took care to make sure we didn't judge Jenny, a single mom, for being a bad parent or "not handling things the right way." She agreed with Jenny that having two people present was better for Davie, and she went on to compliment her friend on her patience and calm demeanor. These two moms understood how much more could be accomplished together by two caring adults, and Davie had the benefit of two people helping one another and caring for him. Cathy and Jenny supported each other over the years, no matter what time of the day or night. They both had children with very serious behavioral issues who benefitted in their relationships with one another, playing together and thinking of each other as family. Cathy, her husband, and Jenny leaned on each other in difficult times, which seemed to be almost nonstop in the early years. Their relationship was the bootstrap that saved them.

RISKING TO CARE

Far too many people have no one in their life who deeply cares about them—no one. This is a reality, and it's often true for people who have been marginalized and who feel lonely, isolated, and powerless. They soon learn that to care about another can mean opening themselves up to great pain. One such person was Janice.

When Janice moved to Hope at age sixty-four, she was friendless, estranged from her children, and without financial security. She was petite, feisty, and fiercely independent, with a gruff veneer protecting her sensitive heart. Asked what brought her to Hope Meadows, she said she thought her own life experiences had prepared her to make a difference in the lives of the children who lived there.

From early childhood into adulthood, hers was a life filled with struggle and loss. Janice grew up in foster care, moving from home to home. She experienced significant abuse along the way. Once I asked where she found the strength to endure so much, especially when she was very young. Janice thought for a while and guessed, "There's an angel somewhere on my shoulder, or maybe God's looking after me." But letting her guard down was difficult, she admitted: "I can get along with everybody. I can be friendly and helpful, but it is very hard for me to get close."[3]

At Hope Meadows people of all ages, abilities, and experiences were encouraged to connect with each other—deeply. Despite her independence and reserve, Janice was not to be an exception. Surrounded by people who genuinely wanted her to be part of their lives and part of the life of the neighborhood, she eventually opened up and let others in, especially Cathy and her family that included six-year-old Ben. Janice became his dearest Hope Grandma.

Knowing what it means to lose everything, Janice worked tirelessly when Hope decided to set up an entire home for a three-generation family of eight made homeless by Hurricane Katrina. She helped fill their pantry with food, contributing jars and jars of her homemade salsa; she donated a bed from her own guest bedroom; and, she made countless trips in her small truck to pick up donations of furnishings for the house.

Janice loved to sew. Not long after she came to Hope, she helped one of the young girls to make a skirt and a jumper. She took great pride in working with "the ladies" (other senior women at Hope) to make quilts for each child at Hope, and in between she created unique cloth dolls which she often gave away. (I will always treasure mine.) Like many at Hope, she loved to garden and bake, and she always shared with neighbors her beautiful cherry tomatoes, green peppers, and delicious homemade breads and cakes.

Janice died six years after moving to Hope. At the memorial service we held for her, Cathy played a DVD showing Janice as a loving, adopted member of their family—celebrating birthdays, playing games, and giving lots of hugs. Many spoke of their friendship with her, and twelve-year-old Ben read this poem he had written for her:

> I love to spend time with Grandma.
> When we fish, she baits the hook.
> She listens to me when I talk.
> And she helps me read my book.
> She gives me hugs and kisses.
> And eats popsicles like a kid.
> I'm really sad that she is gone.
> I love her as much as I ever did.[4]

At Hope Meadows, Janice found not one family but a whole community of everyday people to welcome her, value her many talents and interests, and surround her with caring relationships. The walls she created to protect herself from pain crumbled under the weight of love, friendship and belonging. It was quite a transformation so late in life.

TESTIFYING TO THE POWER OF LOVE

Unlike Janice, some seniors moved to Hope having lived a full and rewarding life that included a good marriage, a loving family, and satisfying work. Jim Saunders was one such fortunate individual. Nonetheless, upon retirement, even with a devoted wife and a strong faith, his life suddenly felt empty. In 1998, in legislative testimony before a State of Illinois Human Services Committee, Jim described how his relationships with the children of Hope Meadows filled this void, giving his life joy, purpose, and meaning. He described a transformative process that redefined what it means to be a family.

It was getting close to noon, and as we were introduced, the legislators—all fifty or so—were shifting in their seats, making ready to "endure" one more presentation. We were given twenty minutes. Jim began:

> Good Morning,
>
> My wife and I were among the first seniors to come to Hope Meadows…almost four years ago. After we retired, we were undecided as to what to do next. You get to a point in your life when you think, 'Well, I am used up. Nothing's left.' But then we got involved with Hope. It was a challenge to work with the children. It has been amazing. It has given us new life. (Gets choked up, clears his throat). I get a little emotional sometimes so just bear with me, but it is so rewarding and gratifying to see the changes in these children and to feel like we have a part in that. We get so involved sometimes. Remember when

Brenda told you that the requirement [for service hours] is six hours per week or twenty-four hours per month? Well, we enjoy this so much that my wife and I put in an average of seventy-five hours per month into the program, and at times we have run close to a hundred. But we ENJOY it!

We see the children come in and realize the needs they have. They are so hungry for love and attention…and we give this freely. I know the primary focus is on the children, but they also make us feel so good because they are concerned about us. I can hardly step outdoors without one of the children asking, 'How is Grandma Mary doing? Is she feeling okay?' When she goes out, they'll do the same and say to her, 'How is Grandpa Jim?'

Once, as we packed the car to go away for a weekend, one of the young boys in the neighborhood came up and in a worried voice asked where we were going and when we were coming back. When we told him our plans, he said, "I'll watch your house for you." Things like that really make you feel a part of something. I know we use the term surrogate grandparents, but I feel like I am more of a member of the family, really. These children are closer to me than my own grandchildren or great-grandchildren because I see them every day, and I get more involved with them.

And then Jim told this story:

When we first moved into Hope, one young man came down and wanted to get acquainted with us. We were out working in the yard when he rode up on his bike. We

> talked a bit, and then he asked, 'Mr. Saunders, can I call you Grandpa?'
>
> I said, 'Sure, you can call me Grandpa.'
>
> He smiled real big, got on his bike, ran back down to his mother, and said, 'Mom, you know, I got more grandpas than anybody else in the whole world.' (Laughter)

At this point in Jim's testimony, we could actually see tears welling up in the eyes of legislators in the room. Jim concluded:

> We have been at Hope, like I said, almost four years, and I have seen other seniors come in like we did, not having any purpose in life, and once they get involved with the children a bond is formed. And you begin to see smiles on their faces, and as they get more involved, it just seems like they get a new shot in the arm. A new life comes into them. And it makes a difference (said with emphasis). It makes a big difference.[5]

Jim said it well, and our twenty minutes expanded into nearly an hour as the legislators first listened then asked lots of questions. They understood that when this retired veteran, his wife, and the children they loved served as grandfriends to one another, their relationships impacted the entire community, bolstering an overall sense of purpose and wellbeing.

Janice and Jim lived in different worlds before coming to Hope, but they had things in common. Both had a strong faith. Both wanted to be useful to others, and both valued their personal independence. Finally, however, as they faced the last years of their lives, both Jim and Janice cast aside their long-held belief in the virtue and necessity of self-reliance, and replaced it with an understanding that we are our best selves, our most joyful, healthy, and resilient selves in relationship with others.

Over time, as residents of all ages continued to experience the personal joy that emerged from their relationships with each other, a culture of care began to permeate the neighborhood. Our visitors could sense it. Many of these visitors were journalists who, having heard from one another about the experiment out on the prairie, began to descend on us. One reporter from a prominent national television news program based in New York City told me wistfully after two days at Hope, "I wish I could raise my children here." When new residents moved in, Hope neighbors stepped in to welcome and to help, like the kids who rushed to shovel Elmer's driveway, and they began straight away to build deep relationships, like the boy who respectfully asked Jim at their first meeting, "Mr. Saunders, can I call you Grandpa?"

For most newcomers, this "neighborliness" was a new experience. How could they not reciprocate? Surrounded by neighbors who cared for them and for their little neighborhood, Jenny, Cathy, Janice, Jim, and so many others at Hope found themselves thinking differently about relationships—in fact, depending upon them—and becoming active participants in the phenomenon David Brooks calls "thick community" and what we came to call *Intentional Neighboring.*

- Eight -

Reframing the Meaning of Vulnerability

> Many different kinds of developments will influence the evolution of vulnerable populations, and among the most influential will be our own values, our beliefs about what is possible, and our efforts to mold the future toward our aspirations.[1]
>
> —Institute for Alternative Futures

At Hope, a second shift in perspective involved a fuller response to vulnerability, rejecting common perceptions of what it means to be vulnerable. We believed that people of any age who face serious challenges that make them vulnerable needed to be first and foremost seen as human beings with the same needs, wants, and desires we all share. We understood, of course, that many of our kids did have special needs; and yes, they did face problems that needed to be addressed; but these were *children*, not problems to be managed.

WE ARE FIRST HUMAN

From the start, *reframing the meaning of vulnerability* became a core value guiding our work at Hope Meadows and "our efforts to mold the future toward our aspirations." We viewed children and other residents experiencing vulnerability through a new lens, one that rejected both widespread beliefs about what it means to be vulnerable and the practices based on these beliefs.

In dictionaries, to be vulnerable is defined as being weak, defenseless, and helpless. In a culture that values independence, individuals who are vulnerable are often viewed as damaged, people who need a great deal of help but who can't offer much to society. They also are seen as problems and as patients or clients always needing professionals to help them. Approaching individuals and their challenges in these denigrating ways creates the worst kind of self-fulfilling prophecy, leading those who are vulnerable to also feel powerless, helpless, hopeless, and without any sense of self-worth.

We rejected these common perceptions and assumptions about vulnerability and worked hard to change them. For us, the very circumstances of vulnerability (which implies a loss of self-determination, be it chronic or acute) required an infusion of the very things that are stripped away when we are judged through a negative lens.

We *valued* those among us who lived with circumstances or conditions which made them vulnerable; they were first and foremost not a problem or burden, but *important and contributing members* of our community, bringing joy and enriching the daily life of our families and of our neighborhood. Ben was a troubled child whose parents abandoned him, but the time he spent with Janice—eating popsicles and fishing together—helped heal her heart and change her life. The adopted children in Elsa's symphony created music not only for her but for our entire community. The kids, no matter how troubled they were, were important and contributing members of our community in another often overlooked or taken-for-granted way. When I think back to when Wayland and I first moved to Champaign not knowing anyone, it was often our kids who helped introduce us to neighbors or to the parents of their friends in daycare—some of whom have remained life-long friends and all of whom helped us to develop a sense of belonging in what was initially a very unfamiliar place. Likewise, it was the children of Hope who almost always were the first to help seniors meet and become friends with the other residents of all ages. What a very important role these children played in bringing newcomers into the fold.

We took care *not* to assume these individuals whom society labeled as vulnerable always needed professionals to make intervention plans and decisions for them; and *not* to define them on the basis of their disability or social challenge, such as being a "foster child." We did not want Kenny, and Sue, and Leon to be pitied, but rather appreciated and honored for the unique children they were. And when older adults such as Esther or Steve had needs due to serious health issues, honoring them with our love, care and assistance brought great satisfaction and joy.

Beyond changing how we viewed people who were vulnerable, we also asked ourselves some challenging questions: "If our own child, parents, or loved ones were viewed through the narrow lens of helplessness and hopelessness, how would we feel?" And, "How might this focus affect the way our loved ones feel about themselves?" As we created policies and made program decisions, we did not first ask what the rules, regulations, and accepted practices told us to do; instead we asked, "Would we be comfortable with our decisions if they were impacting our child, our sister, our parent, our spouse?" This simple exercise caused many of us to rethink our assumptions and reevaluate the practices we had taken for granted as the way things "ought to be;" it caused us to remember and reflect upon what it means to be human first and to have "normal experiences."

The word "normal," is out of favor these days, as we have *finally* gotten more careful about labeling people or circumstances as "abnormal." But we knew that the children who came to Hope Meadows needed to be seen first as ordinary kids requiring the same embeddedness in family and community that any healthy family would work to provide.

Ellen came to Hope at age twelve from a dysfunctional family and a home where sometimes, she told me, the only thing she could find to eat were her crayons. When she was sixteen, she described what normal meant to her.

> For a long time, everyone told me I was just a screwed-up foster child and that I couldn't do anything right.... I guess I got lucky 'cuz now I am living in this cool neighborhood where everyone talks to each other and gets together for barbeques. It's fun and it's safe. I can think of myself as normal here. My Mom says she's proud of me for getting into the National Honor Society, for being in the school play, and for being involved in lots of music stuff at school. I couldn't have done all this before I came here."[2]

Because we determined to respond differently to the people of Hope, we avoided the temptation to focus exclusively on the multiple problems and challenges our children, parents, and seniors faced. Vulnerability did not define them, and as much as possible, we searched for family and community-based practices that valued, empowered and included them. Like Ellen, they never felt excluded from the normal flow of daily life. Without the community and its focus on creating a normative culture of care, our work could easily have failed. Ellen would still have thought of herself as "just a screw-up foster child."

CHANGING EMBEDDED BELIEFS AND PERCEPTIONS

Both residents and staff required education and time to reflect on their own experience of vulnerability. They also needed constant but gentle reminders when they slipped into viewing vulnerability through its conventional lens. We began by letting everyone know the importance of words. Everyone was encouraged to use language that was inclusive and represented "normal." *Labels were the first things to go.* Some families in Hope Meadows—those with previous histories as foster parents—might typically refer to the children who came to live with them as their foster son or daughter. We asked them why. Why didn't they just introduce Mark as Mark or Janelle as Janelle the way they used the first names of their biological children when introducing or referring to them? Wouldn't that be more "normal?"

Likewise, staff and residents were continually reminded not to use terms that would not apply to all children. We cringed if, for example, someone used the term "ward" to refer to a child living at Hope Meadows who had not yet been adopted. Nor did we refer to a home as having a "bed," a child welfare term meaning the space available for a child to be placed there by the state. Would we ever use those terms in reference to a child we had adopted or to whom we had given birth? My children never lived on a "campus" except when they went away to college; they lived in a neighborhood. Nor was our house referred to as a place that had a bed for them; it was a home—*their* home. Our kids lived in our "home," on our "street," in our "neighborhood." And so too, did the children of Hope Meadows. Over and over, we reminded residents inured to the use of social service jargon how the use of conventional, institutional terms *did not reflect our core values,* especially as they related to the most vulnerable among us. The power of language is never so potent as when it strengthens—or undermines—the beliefs that guide us.

We also had to help families understand why certain common practices within the field of child welfare were not acceptable at Hope Meadows. One example is when a family would ask for "respite care." This is a social service term which at Hope meant that parents wanted a child (living in their home but not yet adopted) to be moved to another home for a few days or maybe even a week so they (and others in the family) could have a break from dealing with this child's problem behaviors.

Respite is a widespread practice within the field of child welfare. In reframing what it means to be vulnerable, we asked our Hope families what they would "normally" do when they wanted a break from any of their children *other than* their child still in foster care. Most admitted they might ask a close friend or a family member to take the children for the day, overnight, or for the weekend. They recognized they would never say they needed "respite" but rather something like, "I just need a break for a couple of days."

If our parents needed breathing space or some rest, it was arranged that all or several of their children would spend time away from home, thus removing the stigma associated with singling out the *one* child in foster care. Because of the vast network of relationships at Hope Meadows and the many homes that were licensed to provide care by the State, it was usually quite easy to find a trusted family or families to provide the break a parent needed.

REACTING TO CRISIS

The story of one child—I will call her Sue—offers a compelling example of just how difficult but important it was (and is) to reframe "vulnerability." One day, I returned home in mid-afternoon from several days of meetings out of town. Walking into the house, I immediately picked up the receiver to dial Hope Meadows (this was before cell phones were common)—just to see how things were going in my absence. I was told that Sue had experienced a serious meltdown early in the morning before school, and her parents had called our newest onsite social worker, who came immediately to the family home. She also immediately called a DCFS social worker, per DCFS protocol.

The DCFS worker determined that Sue needed to be admitted to a hospital ward for children with serious emotional problems. She contacted our local facility (twenty minutes away) but it was full and could not admit Sue. Eventually she found a place in a hospital in Chicago, a two-and-a-half-hour drive away. The Hope staff was told that according to the DCFS rules, Sue would have to be transported to the hospital in an ambulance.

When I heard the story—nearly eight hours later—I also learned that the ambulance had yet to arrive! The remaining four children in the home had gone to school that morning and were now coming home. I asked our social worker if one of the parents would be traveling in the ambulance with Sue. "Well," she replied—as if I should know better than to ask—"how would the parent get back home?"

I was angry, frustrated, and heartsick. How could anyone let a child who had endured so much before coming to Hope Meadows and who had just suffered an emotional breakdown, ride alone in an ambulance to a hospital over two hours away? Admission would be traumatic for any child, let alone eight-year-old Sue. Continuing to traumatize an already-traumatized child would be the worst way to handle this situation; it was unthinkable. Never would I want my child to be so abandoned; and never would I leave my child in an ambulance alone—even for a short period of time—unless it was a life-threatening situation and my presence would make the situation worse.

This was a job for the neighbors! I called one of Sue's parents' closest Hope friends, a retired store manager, to ask if she thought the community could step in. She agreed to help, hung up, and got back to me within the hour: everything was arranged. The ambulance had finally arrived—it was after 5 p.m. and already dark outside. The seniors living next door planned to follow the ambulance all the way to Chicago, and then bring Sue's mother back to Hope. Meanwhile other Hope grandfriends would bring pizza for dinner and stay with Sue's siblings until their mom returned. The next morning, they would pick up Sue's siblings, give them breakfast, and take them to school. The seniors were up early anyway, loved having them, and the kids saw it as a special treat. For everyone, once again, this community solution seemed to be a win-win.

WHAT IS AND WHAT SHOULD BE

Despite a satisfactory resolution, the question remained: "Why was Sue treated this way?" The answer is simple: this little girl was still a "ward" of the State, a "foster child." Had her adoption already taken place, everything would have been different.

After the crisis had passed, I reflected on how this day *should* have gone: The social worker, upon arriving at Sue's home in the morning, should have called the neighbors—close friends to Sue and her parents—and asked them to pick up the remaining children and take them to school. This would have set the parents free of all additional responsibilities so they could give their undivided attention to Sue. Another Hope grandparent might have easily been asked to intervene, someone who knew the family well and could help to calm Sue. The social worker could have then truly supported the parents by listening, understanding, evaluating the situation, and helping them to decide what would be best for their daughter.

Yes, DCFS should have been called, but when they arrived, they *would have* found a quieter home and Sue's parents giving their full attention to their child. In that circumstance, immediate hospitalization might not have been the *first* resort. If it were required, Sue should have been accompanied by one or both of her parents, with arrangements made (as they eventually were by Hope residents), for transportation home from the hospital. That Sue would be transported and admitted to the hospital without the support of loved ones should have been out of the question. Again, I ask, why would anyone subject a child to that trauma, especially one as young as Sue and as vulnerable due to previous traumatic experiences? Where was the humanity? Even after so many years, I've found no good answers to these questions. And without answers, practices will not change.

❧

To many DCFS professionals, and for some of our own staff, Hope's policies and practices often bordered on the ridiculous; or at best, were simply wrong because they went against established rules. This was also true for some Hope parents who had been part of the foster care system for so long that changing their views and perceptions of the children and the job of foster parenting was nearly impossible. One experienced foster parent, for example, believed she knew exactly how to parent her troubled foster children—they simply needed "tough love." When her eight-year-old Jessie refused to get out of bed in time to get ready for school, this foster mom would pour cold water on Jessie's face! "That," she said to me with satisfaction, "got her out of bed."

This was one of Hope's most difficult and defining moments. Our policies and practices represented the implementation of our deepest values. Yes, we needed to address deficits and disabilities. And yes, our children needed guidance and discipline. But it was our responsibility to treat those whose challenges made them vulnerable as people we loved and respected. For us, these beliefs were bone deep. Jessie's mom saw her foster child primarily as someone who needed fixing, and she was unable to see and treat her differently. With a heavy heart and hurt feelings on everyone's part, this parent and her family were asked to leave Hope. In their leaving, Jessie had to experience rejection one more time.

Change is never easy, and this is especially true when one is attempting to change embedded beliefs and perceptions. We were able to slowly develop a new culture of care by reframing the meaning of vulnerability. In so doing we were building a neighborhood based on human dignity, self-esteem, and social equity. Over time, the vast majority of Hope's residents grew to see individuals with severe challenges as people first and the problems they faced, as Timothy Shriver writes in *Fully Alive*, as only part of their identities—*not* the whole of who they are.[3] In doing so, we began to think, speak, and act differently. I believe that so engrained in society are our perceptions and practices regarding people who are chronically challenged, that changing this belief system will continue to be—as it was for Jessie's foster mom—a seemingly impossible task. But we must try because, as Susan McFadden writes in *Aging Together*, "No community can flourish unless all of its members, including those who are most vulnerable, also flourish."[4]

- Nine -

Engaging Older Adults: No Small Thing

> Engagement...enhances the health and wellbeing of older adults and creates societal value.[1]
>
> —Zedlewski and Schaner, "The Retirement Project: Perspectives on Productive Aging," *Urban Institute*

The *engagement of our seniors as a way of life* became a third core value at Hope Meadows. Such engagement requires recognizing that older adults represent an expanding but still mostly untapped resource—even, I would argue, an untapped national treasure in helping to support others when they are vulnerable. We didn't know this when we started. Because the needs of the kids and their parents were so intense and numerous, it took me a while to appreciate the profound value of the contributions of our Hope seniors. But eventually we could all see that without the power of their caring presence, Hope Meadows would have become a traditional foster care program at great risk of collapsing under the twin pressures of DCFS rules and the often overwhelming needs of the children.

SIGNIFICANT LIVES

Psychologist Edmund Sanford wrote in 1902:

> The real secret of a happy old age [is to be] once more in service for others carried on to the end of life—a service which, on the one hand, gives perennial interest to life by making the old man a participant in the life of all those about him, and on the other, surrounds him with love in return.[2]

Over a century later, this secret eludes us. As we move into our sixth decade of life and beyond, many of us become physically, socially, and psychologically isolated. The irony is that, like Elmer, we both want and need "to be" engaged, to have purpose in our lives from one day to the next until the end of life.

Retirement and all the ways in which we think about it get in the way of our achieving a "happy old age" in service to others. With the title of old person comes the insidious perception that the old in America are simply not necessary, not useful, and certainly not key contributors to the wellbeing of themselves, others, or society. This idea is wrapped in the common notion of retirement as a time to relax, play, and enjoy our golden years. But even when this life of leisure is feasible for our nation's seniors, such a life is not often satisfying. As Jim and so many others at Hope Meadows told me, "Once we retired, we felt washed up; we no longer had a purpose; we were no longer needed." David Racine put it this way:

> Nothing much is expected of older people. They have no real duties or responsibilities to others. Their significance is largely honorary, like a plaque on the wall—a reminder of the active, productive person they once were. But this is a weak, superficial sort of significance. People's lives have real significance for them only when they are engaged in doing things they and others can regard as significant.

He continues to say,

> What makes Hope Meadows special is that it enables older people to have significance in large part as a function of age. Retirees can do all sorts of things of significance in their communities, but much of the time these things can also be (and often are) done by other, non-retired people as well. Retirees who volunteer in schools, for example, are not providing a service that depends on their age or extensive experience. The service they provide is a good thing. It has significance. But, they do it mainly because they have the time, not so much because of who they are. At Hope Meadows, by contrast, you encourage your older residents to occupy roles and engage in activities that reflect and even amplify their standing as seniors. As a result, their whole lives have significance, not just their specific activities.[3]

Daily at Hope we saw the significance of the lives of our older residents. The seniors were a powerful presence and very important teachers, not only when they were *doing* by being engaged in volunteer activities or dispensing wisdom (often wrapped, as

Dr. Thomas writes, in storytelling), but also by simply *being* and showing us that life, when one is old, can have meaning that is both joyful and profound. Kids who had rarely—or never—known committed couples saw people who had been married for forty or fifty years holding hands as they walked to the community center or enjoyed an evening stroll. They watched people in their seventies and eighties playfully teasing each other at gatherings or laughing as they rode on a fire engine for the first time. Parents, kids, and staff learned from them the value of listening, reflecting, enjoying the smell of rain or a rose in one's garden. We learned the joy of not only doing for others but of *being* with others, telling stories, playing games, or sharing a meal or cup of hot chocolate. And the tangible takeaway was always resilience: if these older people could conquer the hard knocks life had handed them and still be joyful, kind, and grateful, then so could we. The seniors at Hope reinforced our values, providing us each day with clearer insight into what truly makes life worth living for all of us regardless of our differences or how unfair life may sometimes seem. This was a gift no formal system of care could offer.

Elmer Davis's life had significance. In the eulogy I delivered at his memorial service, I said that Elmer taught me all I needed to know about getting old. For nearly ten years after his move from Florida and his appearance on *Nightline*, he did whatever he could for the children who called him Grandpa. He especially enjoyed just having them around. He once said, "The children have done more for us than we have done for them. I've never been happier in my life…I really love being around the children."[4]

During the years Elmer lived at Hope Meadows, he was in and out of the hospital. He needed his pacemaker replaced; he needed a knee replaced; his diabetes continued to give him problems. Each time, I'd visit and ask how long it would be before he came home. "Not long", he'd reply, "I've got to get back to the kids." Elmer understood, as Wendy Lustbader wrote in *Life Gets Better*: "When we know we are making a difference in someone else's life, the body's humiliations matter much less."[5]

I saw this so often. Once, when Elmer was hospitalized, he insisted on an early release so he could travel with Hope kids, parents and other seniors to Seattle. At that time, members of our community were taking yearly holidays to various parts of the United States—all arranged by Anita Hochberger, a senior resident who had retired from a career as a travel agent.

As the person responsible for the wellbeing of our residents on these trips, I worried: "Oh no, Elmer, our trips are fun and educational but they are not easy," I said, thinking to dissuade him, "especially for those of us who are older, like you and me." Did that stop Elmer? Not in the least. With his doctor's permission, Elmer recovered in time for our intergenerational Seattle adventure, despite my concerns.

One year later, just three weeks before he died, he told me how much the trip to Seattle had meant to him and how he would like to go again: "What a good time we had seeing the whales from the boat and everything!" Elmer had lived through hardships, both as a boy growing up during the depression and as an adult working at blue-collar jobs to support his family. This had made him all the more grateful, he told me, for the joy our Hope Meadows community and especially the children had brought him.

Elmer didn't want to let go of that joy. Weeks earlier, he had made an unusual request: When he died, could his ashes be buried near our playground because, he said, "then I will always be near the children."[6]

I was speechless at first, but he'd already talked to Margie, his children and several Hope friends about it—this was important to him. How could his request be denied?

The children loved him too. Here is what Kate, a young African American girl, sixteen at the time of Elmer's death, said at his memorial service:

> Grandpa Elmer was very special to me. Whenever I saw his face it brightened my day, and he always said that I brightened his day too. I always knew that Grandpa gave rides to kids that were running late for school. One day I went to his house to ask if he would take me to band. Immediately he dropped what he was doing and took me. When I got home there was a message on the answering machine from him saying that he had enjoyed taking me to band and that he would take me every day. Every morning from then up to when he started getting sick he would pick me up for school.
>
> I remember one time I was walking home from band when a policeman stopped by and asked me if I had any idea that I was being watched every morning by a white elderly man in a silver car.
>
> I said 'yes.'
>
> 'Did he try to talk to you?'
>
> 'Yes,' I said. 'That man is my Grandpa.'
>
> The policeman immediately started laughing and apologized.
>
> The next morning when I told Grandpa about it, he chuckled and said, 'At least we know they're doing their jobs.'
>
> I always looked forward to hearing him say 'Good

> morning, Sunshine,' and I also was eager each day to hear what he was going to teach me. Every day I learned something new, like for instance, what a slush pump was and why all fire hydrants are not the same color.
>
> We had a lot of good times together. At first, I didn't want to speak at his funeral because it would be too hard for me to say good-bye, but now I realize that I'm only saying good-bye for now on earth because I will see him again in heaven someday, and there you never say good-bye.[7]

In the twenty years he lived in Hope Meadows, Joe Stang, a retired accountant, wholly exemplified David Racine's observations about significance. Joe always had a serious demeanor—a no-nonsense kind of guy. He was incredibly active in the years I was at Hope, but in a quiet way. One neighbor referred to him as a gentle soul. He spent a lot of time with the children on the playground in the summer, and he was always in the community center visiting the kids and talking with other seniors. One mom described how he would ease himself onto the floor to play Twister with her young daughter, and after that, he'd challenge her to a game of checkers.

Joe also contributed to various Hope committees—especially around policy. Once a week he assumed office phone duty, and every year he helped decorate the office for the winter holidays. Nothing was too small or unimportant for him to do. He was a man of faith, and I am told he had many spiritual conversations over the years with a handful of Hope seniors, discussing passages from the Bible.

There was a playful, selfless side to Joe that manifested itself in understated ways. The winter after his wife died, I arrived at

Hope one overcast morning and saw in front of his apartment not just one snowman, but a family of snow people—father, mother, and two kids. Joe told me he thought the children would enjoy them. It may not seem like a big thing, but to me, and to the entire Hope community, it showed how much he cared. This little snow family, on an otherwise cold and dreary day, brought smiles to our faces regardless of our age.

One year, only days before we were to be in the annual Rantoul July 4th parade, we asked Joe if he would be Uncle Sam on the Hope float. He hesitated, then finally agreed. As we were gathering to line up in the parade, here he came. To our surprise and delight, he was dressed in an Uncle Sam costume he'd rented on his own, without telling anyone. He looked—and was—*perfect* for the part!

Joe's main volunteer "task" at Hope Meadows was to be a crossing guard. He liked the job because of the routine. It gave him a reason, he said, to get out of bed every morning. His main concern was the safety of the children as the sidewalk they took to get to school was next to a field of corn which, in the fall in Illinois, grew very tall indeed. Joe looked out for and mentored the Hope children and other children that crossed his path on a daily basis. He was a good listener and very observant. One senior commented, "Joe worked hard as a crossing guard. Young kids followed him right up to his front door, like a Pied Piper."[8]

Rob Gurwitt, in his 2002 article, "Fostering Hope," written for *Mother Jones* magazine, spent a morning in the community with Joe, and writes:

> At the Hope playground one sunny morning, Joe Stang is playing ball with a small knot of Hope children. He is a tall man with silver hair and a toothy smile that

veers toward the sardonic. Among Hope's seniors he has a reputation as a curmudgeon, though with the kids he is a patient, sturdy presence. He has been paying special attention to a seven-year-old boy named Keith—Gary's adoptive brother—who collapses in dramatic wails whenever he misses a ball or gets confused. "Keith," Joe keeps reassuring him, "we're just practicing here, so we learn for later."

Eventually, Keith hits a pop-up, throws the bat down, stomps off, and again starts crying. "Keith, Keith, I want to show you something," Joe says, following him. "I want to show you how to do it better so next time it'll go better." He shows Keith how to swing, drop the bat, and run to first. Keith can't seem to shake his own dark mood and turns away, but then changes his mind and picks up the bat. He hits a mighty double, and, yelling happily, rounds the base to second, then heads for home. His triumph is short-lived. Next time up, he hits the ball again, runs to first, then hesitates. By the time he decides to run to second base another boy, Stuart, is waiting with the ball and tags him out. He wails, wanders off the field, and sits down. Joe Stang follows, sits next to him, and starts in again, talking softly.

A year ago, when Keith arrived at Hope Meadows with two of his birth sisters, this ball game would have been impossible. He grew up in a setting rife with alcoholism; his mother had seven children with several different men, one imprisoned for killing two of Keith's half siblings. Keith couldn't laugh when he got here. Nor did he know how to interact with other people, or how to show his emotions in any but the most angry and dramatic ways.

> That he's sitting still, letting Joe Stang talk calmly with him, is no small thing.[9]

Joe's value to all of us was no small thing. As his story and Elmer's illustrate, the engagement of older adults touched every corner of our daily lives and produced powerful and positive results. It strengthened everyone's commitment to the neighborhood; catalyzed the formation of long and meaningful relationships; enhanced the seniors' status as older adults; and encouraged, on a daily basis, their *giving back* and *making a difference.*

Engagement became a way of life, filling the last years and decades of a senior's life with real meaning, purpose, and joy. Far from retreat or isolation, they built stronger relationships daily, across three generations. These people grew to recognize their immense value as they offered us gifts of knowledge, wisdom, and skills acquired through a lifetime of experience. They felt a sense of belonging and communion—rooted in place. The entire neighborhood provided them with a *human safety net*, often eliminating the need for services from the broader community. They could count on help with life-course transitions, especially through retirement, old-old age, and the death of a spouse.

One unanticipated outcome—something I believe rarely happens in old age—was that life for our Hope seniors became oriented to the future. Author Wendy Lustbader captures the essence of this phenomenon when she writes: "Generosity calls us to life. Involvement in the lives of others is ever replenishing, while pining for self-fulfillment drains the spirit."[10] Grandparents know this to be true. So too did seniors like Jim who dearly cared about their "Hope grandchildren." Instead of falling into despair because life was purposeless or close to being over, Hope seniors looked forward to the promise of sharing life with others: "I have to help Angel learn to drive." "I'm looking forward to seeing Johnny graduate." "I'm taking Mary to a play next week." Seniors not only anticipated the future, they woke up every day ready to be present and available to the parents, to one another, and—most especially—to the children. As David Racine so poignantly describes, they were integral in sustaining the rhythms of day-to-day community life:

> At the beginning of the day, during the heart of the day, and at the end of the day older adults provide a web of familiarity, continuity, trust, belonging, encouragement, and hope for the entire community. The integration of older adults is not just a "nice" thing, but "necessary" to the amelioration of social problems within the community. The ready availability and engagement of older adults reduces the stress families may experience caring for children and managing their households, thereby enhancing family functioning. Older adults form the bedrock of social connectedness and communal participation, both powerful determinants of individual and community wellbeing.[11]

Here David makes a crucial point. Not only is engagement and its resulting connectedness good for healthy aging, *it is necessary to the amelioration of social problems* within the community. Not only do the seniors and other residents facing social problems benefit; social services also benefit. When the intergenerational neighborhood is doing its job, the formal service systems around it are less pressed and more capable of making a difference. *Intergenerational relationships formed through community engagement provide what traditional services cannot: a context for eliciting and sustaining attachment, trust, and a strong sense of safety and belonging.* These complementary functions can reduce the burden on social services, providing a strong human partnership in the work to address even the most intractable problems.

A SENIOR WORKFORCE, A FORCE OF LOVE

For the work of the community to be done effectively, a large representation of senior residents was necessary. At Hope Meadows we found the ratio of three to four senior households to each family household to be optimal. The following senior engagement data, covering a six-month period during our second year of operation, provide a glimpse of how much they contributed to the betterment of the Hope community and to the operation of our nonprofit organization. Seniors logged a total of 9,270 volunteer care hours. Nearly two-thirds of these hours were spent in direct work with children. Every month we saved $3,000 in expenses that we would otherwise have had to pay. Seniors answered phones in the office, performed custodial work, assisted with building maintenance and repairs, helped in keeping the grounds looking nice, and more. Some of their weekly jobs included working in the library, reading to children, caring for kids whose parents were in training classes, helping children get to and from school, monitoring the playground, participating in the afterschool program and delivering the latest copy of our weekly newsletter, *Seedlings,* to every home.

This level of planned engagement did not just happen. It was jumpstarted by policies and practices based on our core values. We required all older adults to participate weekly in a minimum of six hours of caring engagement both formally, such as tutoring or planning an afternoon activity, and informally, such as inviting children in for cookies and milk or fixing a child's bike when he stopped by after school.

We also provided physical and material support, including reducing the going rate for rent by $100 per month and modifying housing so it was more easily accessible for older adults. This was in recognition of, or some might say "in exchange" for the required hours of community engagement. Decoupling the amount of benefit received, such as reduced rent from the amount of engagement, seemed to work in unexpected ways. Everyone appreciated the cheaper cost of housing. In exchange for this "bonus," they were more than willing to provide service hours, and in most households, this translated into lots of hours. But no one thought they were getting "paid" or that each hour they gave to the children and the community was worth a certain dollar amount. The board and staff did all we could through policies and practices to prevent commodification, the viewing of our children as sources of income.

Initially we had no policies or formal documentation around required engagement. It had simply been understood (and written in their lease) that Hope expected each senior household to give the community six hours a week of their time. By the time I became director of Hope Meadows at the start of its third year, tensions around issues of fairness and accountability had emerged. We called a meeting with the seniors, and I began what I thought would be a difficult conversation by acknowledging the importance of each of their roles in the lives of the children and families at Hope. I wanted them to know just how important they were. I then asked them to talk among themselves and appoint one or two people to present sample policies about how to account for their hours. Most were ready and willing!

As they worked to reach consensus, it became clear that

planned and more formal activities would count as service hours, but simply attending events like a picnic or meeting would not—unless the person had put in some time planning or organizing the event. They also agreed that six hours per month spent unplanned or informally with a child or children *would* count. For a few seniors—there were always some who tended to take advantage of reduced rent without putting in the required hours of engagement—these new policies did not sit well, and most of those people eventually moved away. For the vast majority, however, the new policies were welcomed expectations of justice and accountability, helping us all to confirm our intentions as a community of care and kindness.

Over the years these policies evolved to consider the changing needs and abilities of our seniors and included a reduction in required hours of service. Seniors could be considered vested if they had lived at Hope Meadows for fifteen years, or if they had accumulated five thousand service hours and reached age seventy-seven. We realized that seniors might not be able to fulfill their commitment because of an illness or hospitalization. Or maybe they had to be away due to family matters related to their adult children, or they simply wanted to spend a few weeks or a month on vacation. Finally, seniors established a banking system whereby they could accumulate extra hours to be used at a later time. These hours also could be loaned to a neighbor who might be unable to fulfill the obligations for reduced rent, reflecting yet another way for neighbors to help one another in our community.[12] Joe Stang, who helped design this banking system, named it "Hope's Treasure Chest."

Like us all, Hope seniors possessed unique personalities and temperaments, strengths and weaknesses; this contributed to their engagements not always being trouble-free. Some people were more present and *vocal* about the good things they were doing. Others, like Joe Stang, worked behind the scenes, doing great things quietly. These differences sometimes led to jealousy, envy, and—once in a while—resentment, which also once in a while led someone who had donated many loaner hours to the "bank" to want some "say in the matter" about who should or should not receive them. Everyday people aren't saints, after all. I smile as I write this, thinking of the individuality of each senior (making us a *normal* community) and how—in spite of differences, irritations and human imperfections—the contributions of each individual, no matter the focus or magnitude, when put together, made a powerfully effective and wonderfully diverse whole.

Engagement as a way of life for older adults is very different from the typical *lifestyle* in retirement communities. Most of these communities are age restricted, places where residents must be at least fifty-five and partially or fully retired. Usually, children are allowed to visit but are not allowed to be residents. Diversity is uncommon, not only in age, but in household income, and often in the way people think. Engagement in the life of the community is not required; instead, the focused lifestyle is often leisure—centering on a shared interest or hobby such as golf. Rarely, if ever, is the primary focus on living supportively with neighbors.

Unlike these typical retirement communities, the specific social challenge to be addressed by the seniors at Hope Meadows and their commitment to community engagement became the main reason for living there. It was the focal point for organizing their work on behalf of the neighborhood, and it became a fundamental source of identity and cohesion, making individual differences an asset. No longer did seniors feel used up or lonely. They were valued for the wisdom, independence, experience, humor, and curiosity they shared through daily engagement, not only for the betterment of Hope Meadows, but for the betterment of society.

As seniors made the transition from family and work life to retirement, engagement provided the necessary context and structure as a new lifestyle emerged for them and as shared purpose began to give meaning to their lives. Miss Irene, one of the first seniors to move to Hope Meadows, may have said this best when she echoed the words of Edmund Sanford:

> You are never alone here. All the love they have, they give to you. You give out love and you get it back. Sometimes you ask yourself, 'why am I here?' Because you are getting older and you are tired, but then you put your head on the pillow in the night time and you know that you made a little child happy.[13]

When that little child is someone like Kenny, Sue, or Keith, making them happy, as Rob Gurritt observes, is "no small thing."

- Ten -

Doing Life Together

> I've found immense solace the last two days in working on the Hope piece: Just a little corner where people are trying in small ways to make the world a better place.[1]
>
> —Journalist, visiting Hope on 9/11 in a letter to its residents

The three guiding values related to caring relationships, reframing vulnerability, and engagements of older adults were at the core of Hope's being. They were reflected in daily acts of care, celebration, tradition-building, and helping—people being there for one another in difficult times. Individual acts of kindness rarely went unnoticed, and we made sure to express our gratitude in public ways. We celebrated whenever and whatever we could—holidays, birthdays, anniversaries, adoption days, milestones of every kind, the people we loved, and the little victories and transformational moments that marked our lives. These celebrations and the traditions we created around them involved the entire community and happened regularly. And as for people helping people when they needed it most? Well, that was simply expected.

SPECIAL AND EVERYDAY ACTS OF CARE

Twelve-year-old boys don't often write poetic tributes to the people they have loved and lost. Ben's poem honoring his beloved Grandma Janice was a special act of care taking much time, thought, and planning. Posted on our community center bulletin board for all the community to see, it drew much praise for his writing and his thoughtfulness. In his young and fractured life, such praise and attention were unfamiliar to Ben; coming from so many Hope friends and grandfriends, it was a gift of encouragement he would never forget.

In this regard, the importance of positive memories shouldn't be underestimated. Lizbeth Schorr, in a book she authored on breaking the cycle of disadvantage, quoted Father James Harvey, a priest who helped many young men who came to him from their worlds of crime and violence. He said, "These youngsters come in, they don't have food, they don't have clothes, many of them don't have a place to sleep.... People [ask], what is the biggest thing they don't have. And I believe it's memories. These young people have no good memories of the past."[2]

These notes, kudos, and acknowledgements of special acts of care were also printed in our *Seedlings* newsletter. One resident wrote what all of us felt after a couple in the neighborhood generously hosted a Christmas dinner for Hope residents: "The table was set beautifully, the food was great, and the companionship with everyone there was priceless. It made not being able to be with family easier." Someone else in that same issue wrote, "Congratulations to the Hope staff, kids, and seniors who helped decorate the snowman for the competition held by the Rantoul Chamber of Commerce. It won first place!"[3]

Not all acts of care were quite so magnificent. In fact, most of our everyday caring involved small gestures of great kindness, and we learned to express our gratitude for them as often and as openly as we could. Miss Irene wrote once to thank James for stopping by as he was riding his bicycle to tell her to get off her knees and sit in a chair while he finished planting her tulip bulbs. Grandma Vera wrote thanking two small children for stopping by to help her sort books in the library. Seniors often wrote to thank a child who helped them to walk home after a party at the playground or our community center. In each of these examples, the greatest gift was in the noticing, a relational skill our Hope children developed as well as any adult.

When a beloved grandparent died, the children often expressed their love and grief in ways that would surprise and touch any of us. Bill (Esther's self-appointed chauffeur and chef) and his wife Fran moved to Hope Meadows in 1994. Ten years later, Bill died of heart and liver disease two months before his sixty-seventh birthday. At his funeral, two of his Hope grandchildren served as pallbearers, and another read a poem she and her mother had written together, entitled *Grandpa Bill.* Following the funeral, kids gathered at the community center and decided to write sympathy notes to Grandma Fran. This was not the staff's idea. Once finished, they walked in groups of three across the street to her house to deliver them, saying they thought she would be sad and lonely. Fourteen years later, Fran still has these handwritten notes, and she often speaks of them with tears in her eyes. Here are just two of many she received:

> Dear Grandma Fran,
>
> We are sorry for the loss of Grandpa Bill. We liked Grandpa Bill very much and we're very sad that he died. We really miss spending time with him while he was sick. We will miss the times he spent Christmas caroling with

us and doing things with us. We liked when
would let us help him around the house. We really
talking to him and just having fun with him. We love you, and we hope you know that Grandpa is still here with us. We love you, and we want you to know that God is by your side all the time.

Jessie (age thirteen) and Shalyn (age five)

Dear Grandma Fran,

I want you to know that if you need anything you can call on me. I am very sorry for his death. If you need a liver or something, I'll find you one. That's all I can do. But anyway, if you want to talk about anything, you can call me. If you need help moving...anything, call me.

Sincerely, Calvin (age twelve)[4]

CELEBRATION AND TRADITION

Hope celebrations almost always became annual events, becoming traditions in and of themselves. But traditions evolved inside of every celebration as well—special ways of doing things, awards, songs, activities. All acts were meaningful, creating in our midst a tapestry of belonging, continuity, and security—a story in which each person, young and old, and the neighborhood as a whole mattered. Traditions brought generations together, helping us to connect to our past and celebrate the present.

WELCOME TO HOPE

We honored and celebrated one another right from the start. When new parents or seniors arrived, we ran a "Getting Acquainted" column in *Seedlings*. This included personal details about work and family, special experiences or funny stories, and skills and preferences. Again, no secrets were safe with us. When Mr. James arrived, we all learned that he enjoyed fishing, watching old movies on television, and that he possessed an especially green thumb. It wasn't long before he was working with another resident, planting flowers and pulling weeds. They became great friends, and Hope became a much prettier place.

HOLIDAYS AT HOPE

Holiday gatherings were especially well-attended. Food was plentiful and we took special care to create lasting traditions unique to our neighborhood, knowing the memories they would build. Months old in 1994, Hope celebrated its very first holiday together with a July 4th picnic, complete with a visit from the Rantoul fire department, dressed for action and ready with sirens roaring to give anyone who wanted a ride around the block. Adventurous seniors, including me, rode a fire truck for the first time! We also constructed a Hope Meadows float and proudly entered it in the Rantoul Independence Day parade. These traditions continued, and we amassed quite a few first-place trophies for our floats over the years, including the year Joe participated as Uncle Sam.

Hope's annual Halloween costume party and wiener roast was a riot, a time when seniors, parents, and staff dressed in costumes alongside the children. One year I dressed as a witch, complete with a green face, a long clay nose, and a crazy wig, and I was so convincing no one recognized me for hours! We held an annual winter party too, and an Easter egg hunt in the spring.

Because holiday celebrations were so popular, the seniors who gathered weekly to work on quilts decided to create a new tradition of presenting a handmade quilt to one or two kids at every holiday celebration. Each quilt was unique, mindfully designed to reflect a child's favorite color and special interests, such as baseball or teddy bears. The Hope staff supported this resident-led initiative by providing tables, sewing machines and a gathering space for quilting. Both staff and the entire community took pride and much pleasure in seeing the joy on a child's face when she was presented—in front of everyone—with a quilt made especially for her.

ONLY AT HOPE

The community wholly embraced more traditions, both suggested and organized by residents. Every summer we hosted our very own week-long sports camp for the kids with parents and seniors supervising. (It was at one of these sports camps where Joe Stang coached Keith.) A second tradition (and my favorite) was the Annual Ladies Tea Party. Every day for a week, teams of senior women and moms would work to transform the dining area of our community center into an elegant Victorian tea room; each woman took a table, decorating it with fresh flowers, their own china place settings, and special tablecloths—all reflecting the theme chosen for that year. Then, on Saturday afternoon, ladies of all ages dressed in their finery, complete with hats and gloves and gathered for an afternoon of tea, entertainment, and companionship. The program included songs and poems, some of them written by Hope residents. To watch our smiling, beautiful girls—knowing what their lives had been like prior to Hope—drinking tea poured from delicate china pots and eating cucumber sandwiches—that was magical indeed.

HONORING LIVES

Not all celebrations were joyful. When we began, we couldn't imagine what the deaths of our residents would mean to us. We lost Larry unexpectedly, and many more seniors over the years. We could not have known that while each death would be a deeply-felt loss, the traditions we created at Hope to honor our loved ones would become some of our most cherished memories and bring all of us together in ways nothing else could. When a resident died, we honored him or her in the next issue of *Seedlings* along with information about any official services. We also held our own celebration of a treasured life at Hope Meadows. We filled the community center with pictures, notes and poems like the one Ben wrote, in order to keep that person in our minds and hearts. One resident wrote this note about Janice which said, in part, "We enjoyed arguing with each other—so who will argue with me now? She will always have a special place in my heart."

When Miss Esther passed away, one child with a deeply troubled past wrote this note for the community to read:

> Grandma Esther was my first grandma when I moved to Hope. She was my tutorer [*sic*] and she was my friend. We used to have tea parties with our American Girl dolls. We used to bake cookies all the time. I would take half and she had half. We went to the store to run arons [sic]. On Mother's Day we would give her a present. I will always remember her as my Hope Grandmother.[5]

Mr. Lee was one of our younger seniors, a retired steelworker with a warm smile and as one parent said of him, "He was a man of wisdom; a friend to all. He was a mentor to many; a pal to the small." When he died suddenly, just a few hours after sharing morning coffee with his neighbors, Al wrote this verse in his memory.

I said goodbye to Mr. Lee.
I've lost my good buddy, my pal, my friend.
Will the shock and the pain ever end?
We would meet for coffee most every day,
or sit in his carport and watch the kids at play.
A kinder, truer, friend I'll never know.
It is hard for me to have to let him go.
But my memories of him will stay with me.
As they will with all who knew Mr. Lee.
In the words of my granddaughters as they walked with me,
'Papa, I waved and said goodbye to Mr. Lee.'[6]

Who knew Al was a poet or that he had such deep feelings for his friend?

At our Celebration of Life services held at Hope, we gathered to tell stories, and maybe a child would sing a song or read something she had written as Kate did at Elmer's service. We always displayed photos taken at Hope over the years. There was plenty of food too. To honor Mr. Lee, Kenny Calhoun (Hope's go-to chef, father of many adopted children, and Mr. Lee's dear friend) fried batches and batches of chicken wings—Mr. Lee's favorite food—for all of us to enjoy.

HAPPY BIRTHDAYS

At Hope we recognized birthdays. Each month, one of the seniors would make an events' calendar noting planned activities, holidays, and all birthdays. Every Monday, a list would appear again in *Seedlings* to remind residents of those having a birthday that week, and once a month we'd have a community party to celebrate everyone whose birthday fell during that time. One highly creative and ingenious senior even created a Birthday Pole, based on a

May Day Pole, with lots of ribbons and balloons attached. On the day of any resident's birthday, a senior would sneak over and place the pole in his or her front yard—special recognition, no matter whether one was turning eight or eighty! (This was one of those official volunteer tasks counting as part of service hours, so the senior benefited too.) Every morning as I drove through our twenty-acre neighborhood to get to my office, I'd look for that pole with its bright ribbons blowing in our Illinois prairie wind. What a way to brighten everyone's day—mine, the morning crossing guards headed to their posts, the children walking to school, and the early-rising seniors making their way to the community center for morning coffee! No one's birthday was ever a secret at Hope.

I've heard it said that anticipation is the electricity of childhood; this was especially true for our Hope children. Our community celebrations were not only fun, (or in the case of memorial celebrations, poignant), they helped to cement the children's otherwise fragile sense of safety and belonging. For every child placed in the foster care system, this sense of security and any hope of a predictable world is shattered. Our children were purposefully included in the making of community celebrations, giving us all joy and helping them to know they were finally in a place where they were accepted, cared about, and safe—a place where they belonged.

Traditions are especially important to families and to children, but for many of the children we cared for at Hope, the joy of traditions had often been marred by abuse. I've heard lots of horror stories over the years, but one that always sticks with me involves a precious tradition hijacked for the emotional abuse of a four-year-old boy. He came to Hope from foster care with his five- and six-year-old siblings, and we were told he was not well-liked by his "foster parents." Apparently, the Christmas before he arrived at Hope, he and his brother and sister jumped out of bed to see what was under the tree, where they found gifts for his siblings but *none* for him. His foster parents told him he had been a bad boy and Santa does not bring toys to bad boys!

We all worked hard to practice traditions in ways that healed rather than harmed our children. For this boy, a typically harmless Santa myth was weaponized by the very people in charge of his wellbeing. The message was indelibly printed on his heart: he was not only a bad boy, but so bad as not to be worthy of even Christmas joy. I can only hope that his time at Hope helped to reverse that message.

We reinforced our values not only by acknowledging acts of kindness and through celebrations and traditions, but in the expectation that people of all ages would rally to assist neighbors in need. One parent might come to the aid of another, as Cathy and Jenny routinely did. What we heard about most often were stories of neighbors caring for people when they were ill. Sometimes this support was incredibly well-coordinated. When Jack came down with pneumonia, one of the seniors helped him to gain admittance to the Veteran's hospital while another senior transported him to the hospital and brought him back home once he was released. This hospital was a forty-five-minute drive from Hope Meadows. While Jack was in the hospital and then home in recovery, the neighbors made sure he and his wife Alice had plenty of food on the table. What surprised Alice the most was that the food kept coming two and three weeks later!

One winter, the entire Calhoun family came down with the flu. One day there was a knock on the door. Kenny, sick himself, opened it to find his neighbor, donning a surgical face mask and holding a huge bag of oranges. "I'm not coming in." he said as he held his arm out to hand Kenny the bag. "I just thought you and the kids could use an extra dose of Vitamin C. These oranges may help all of you feel better." And off he went.

The children, too, were sensitive to the needs of others and often wanted to help. Sometimes that meant creating cards or gifts for someone who was sick. Helen recalled that after she had had surgery the children next door made her a get-well card. She described it as hand-drawn with crayon from the kids. It read, "Just for you. We know you have not been yourself since you had your little stitch. So, we send you this card to help you ignore that itch! We love you, Grandma Helen." The card was signed by all eight members of the family, and a picture accompanied each signature. On the back was written, "Prayerfully created by children's love."[7]

These acts were a regular part of "doing life together" at Hope, and the news of them spread around the neighborhood quickly at daily morning coffees, potlucks, and community-wide celebrations. Whenever I heard about them, I'd find someone to give me the details, and then spread the news myself, knowing that in the telling of these stories, we were constructing an oral history of Hope and a guide to our future. I think almost everyone felt this way. Acts of care and kindness soon multiplied with the result that everybody took pride in what neighbors had done for one another and the importance of the intergenerational relationships they had made. They recognized that because of these deeply caring relationships, they belonged to something bigger than themselves.

Part IV

THE POWER OF THE PEOPLE NEXT DOOR

- Eleven -

From Intervention to Intentional Neighboring

> Vision is the basic building block of new communities.... Having a vision is different from having a plan.... A vision catches the spirit of a people. It never identifies how something will happen.[1]
>
> —Beth Jarman and George Land
> "Beyond Breakpoint: Possibilities for New Community"

When I reflect upon my life I often think in decades—how my life changed and what my major purpose or sense of identity was when I was in my twenties, thirties, forties, and fifties. Each decade seems to embody a specific transition. In my twenties I married; in my thirties I had my children and finished graduate school; in my forties I conducted research on adoption; and in my fifties I started Hope Meadows, which, in its first decade, focused on creating new families and reinventing intergenerational community. After ten years, most of the children were adopted and families were no longer worried that DCFS might take their children away. The seniors, too, had their routines, close friendships, and strong sense of purpose. Everyone, it seemed, was beginning to take this close-knit neighborhood for granted. Finally I could let my guard down, thinking it might be time to take life just a little easier. But that was not what happened.

In the fall of 2004, Marty and I went to Chicago for a two-day forum on children aging out of foster care. We sat through a day and a half of talks, but with each session I became more disillusioned. Expert speakers highlighted critical challenges faced by these children in their transition to adulthood—access to housing, employment, job training, and continuing education, to name a few. But not one of them mentioned the devastating loss of supportive relationships—except the kids themselves. To a person, these vulnerable, courageous young people stood up on stage to tell us that the hardest part of leaving foster care was that they had no one to turn to, no one to help them as they faced the world, when, for the first time, they were expected to be adults and totally responsible for themselves. They said it over and over, on panels and in presentations, but it seemed to fall on deaf ears.

By noon on the second day of the forum, I'd had enough and just wanted to get the sessions over with and leave. Marty and I picked up the boxed lunches provided to us and stood at a counter to eat. I was tired and not in the mood to network or to engage in small talk. But as we ate our sandwiches, one of the attendees joined us and introduced himself as Ted Chen of the W.K. Kellogg Foundation. To be polite, I told him my name and that I was with Generations of Hope (we had changed our name from Hope for the Children by then), a nonprofit that focused on getting children adopted from foster care. To facilitate these adoptions, we had created a small community to provide the adoptive families with support. I told him I was disappointed that all we had heard so far at the forum were the problems kids aging out of foster care were facing. Why weren't solutions ever offered at such gatherings? Having said enough, I turned back to my sandwich.

Marty urged me on whispering, "Brenda, tell Ted more!" but the forum had done me in and I simply couldn't muster the energy to go into depth about Hope Meadows. I did offer to send him some printed information about our work if he was interested.

Ted smiled and handed me his card, "Please do."

We parted. Marty and I attended closing sessions and headed for home. A few days later and without much thought, I sent off the packet I'd promised. When I heard back from Ted one month later, I was in court observing Dwayne's first trial for murder.

It was a grueling day of testimony. During a much-welcomed recess, I phoned the Hope office and, to my surprise, was told Ted had just called to speak with me. With only a few minutes before the trial resumed, I quickly returned his call. Ted thanked me for the information I'd sent him, asked questions that I know I answered but cannot now recall, and promised to call back in a few days. This he did, to request I write a proposal for funding from Kellogg to take our work in new directions. This national foundation wanted to see if we could replicate what we were doing at Hope Meadows. And so began my sixth decade of life!

Our proposal was accepted, and we did receive funding. Four months later I said a tearful goodbye to the wonderful, inspiring people of Hope Meadows and moved my office to Champaign to direct a national replication effort. I looked forward to a new challenge and to working with Ted, but my heart ached. How I would miss these people. They meant so much to me. For ten years I had listened to and recorded their stories, both joyful and sad. Together we had celebrated triumphs and learned from our failures; we had practiced daily kindnesses even in the midst of community disagreements or of grief at the loss of a loved one. These deeply caring people had taught me so much, and they would always have a place in my heart.

A NEW DECADE, A NEW BEGINNING

Ending that chapter of my life, my colleagues who had helped to write the Kellogg proposal—Marty, David Hopping, David Racine, and Elissa Thomann Mitchell—began to work with groups and organizations around the country wanting to adapt what had been developed at Hope Meadows. One of our first tasks was to help them understand that what was emerging was a neighborhood model based on our core values and offering *both a place to live and a new program structure for social intervention.* Our central claim was this: by cultivating a network of caring intergenerational relationships within a geographically contained area, the solving of problems related to vulnerability can shift from *intervention within community* to *community as intervention.*

In this new intervention paradigm, ordinary people—*the people next door*—provided extraordinary levels of neighboring within the normal course of daily living. Unlike conventional intervention practices in which professional services are designed to meet a specific challenge and produce a well-defined outcome, for us, successful intervention depended upon caring relationships with neighbors and staff. The overarching challenge was to empower neighbors to become masters of care and kindness in addressing one another's needs, especially those of the most vulnerable. We began to refer to this model as *Intergenerational Community as Intervention,* or ICI for short.

A NEW ORGANIZATIONAL CAPACITY

Integral to ICI were the volunteers who, at Hope Meadows, were primarily older adults like Elmer, Joe, and Miss Irene. When added to social services, volunteer programs are typically designed to reduce the burdens of service professionals, supporting and allowing them to provide interventions they are trained and paid to do. Figure 1 illustrates this traditional practice. The three diagrams that follow represent our transition to a new kind of organizational capacity.

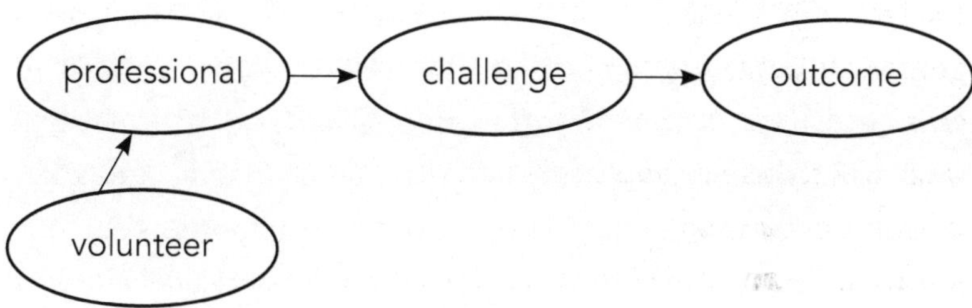

Figure 1. Typical service configuration

In the ICI concept, it was not the presence of volunteers that was new, but the central role they played in addressing social problems and ultimately in increasing organizational capacity.

Over time, neighbors began to often take it upon themselves to identify and fulfill a need. This might be as simple as taking food to someone because they were sick, or assuming crossing guard duties for another senior—as Margie did, while Eileen went out of state on a family matter. "She asked me," Margie told us, "so that's what I did." Staff never got involved in finding a substitute for Eileen. Instead, several residents jumped into action. Margie always said her best memories of living at Hope "come from the fact that whenever we need somebody, someone is always there." She told this story:

> When they first found out that Elmer had cancer, they would take him down to the chemo and down to the radiation clinic. I just think it's one of the greatest things because I lived in a small community when I grew up, and that's the way it was then. At one of the morning coffees, someone started a signup sheet. They said anybody that wanted to sign up could sign up. We started out with nine drivers—now we have fifteen! They just want to *do* for us.[2]

Margie was soft spoken and gentle, and she somehow seemed frail to me. Her neighbor Joan, who had never lived in a small town until moving to Rantoul, was in no way fragile and could sometimes have what one might call "sharp elbows." But like Margie, Joan was a doer and was always involved in a new project helping her neighbors, the kids, or planning a community-wide activity or celebration. She tutored children, taught many kids to tap dance in the after-school program, planned fabulous Martin Luther King celebrations; she was always there when her neighbors needed help.

Joan once said, "I love the fact we are a community. We really are.... Unlike in Chicago, here I just walk out of my house and start talking to people. When people move here, we just gather them in. We do for them and [like Margie said] they do for us."[3]

This is what happened to Joan, a retired school teacher, the day she moved to Hope. A neighbor whose husband was a retired laborer and whose race and life experiences were different from Joan's, stopped in, introduced herself, and said, "Here, why not use my phone until your phone is connected."

Joan knew immediately that Hope was a new kind of neighborhood. "In Chicago, I know I would never give my phone to a person I did not know. But Alice was so very friendly and so helpful. Later on, when she needed help, it was just my turn, you know?"

Like so many acts of neighborliness, the staff often learned of this "doing for each other" after the fact. We were thrilled that Elmer's neighbors had themselves organized transportation for his medical appointments, and we loved hearing stories of how Alice and Joan supported one another. As "doing for each other" became part of the ethos of Hope Meadows, the residents began to see themselves less as formal volunteers, and more like neighbors making a difference. Figure 2 below illustrates this service configuration.

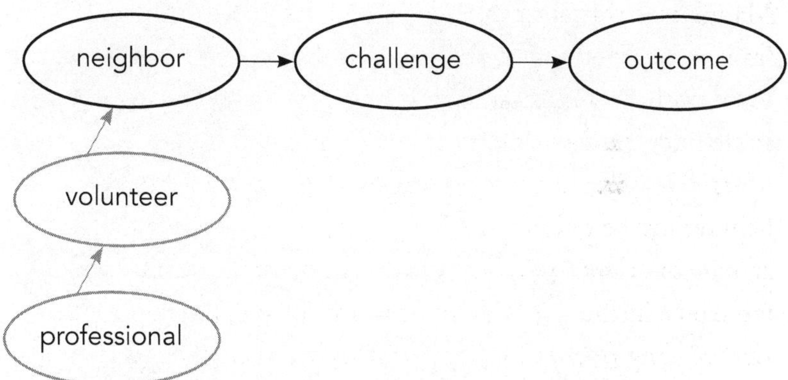

Figure 2. Hope service configuration

Moreover, the volunteers began to assume multiple roles. They were already neighbors, but they became friends, and friends often became mentors, and mentors might become "grandparents." Similarly, the children who were initially seen primarily as victims of abuse and neglect, as they engaged with the seniors, also acquired new roles: that of neighbor, friend, helper, mentee, and grandchild. Within their adoptive families they simply became sons and daughters, brothers and sisters. Ultimately, as both the traditional roles of on-site professional staff and volunteers receded into the background, a new form of organizational capacity emerged (*Figure 3*) where the neighbors, in their new roles, took on a dominant position in meeting challenges and producing outcomes.[4]

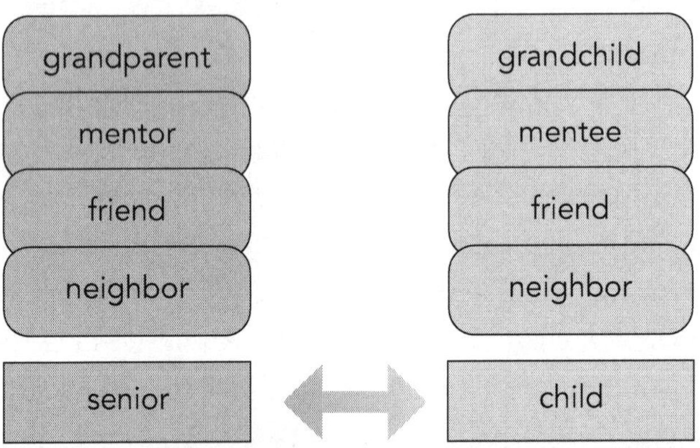

Figure 3. Multistranded Relations

In this new model of intervention, neighboring became the first line of support and service, a familiar concept to many who've grown up in highly connected, old fashioned neighborhoods. While augmenting professional services, this approach shifts the initial focus of problem solving from professional service providers to members of the community. David Racine has gone so far as to suggest this strategy "is primary and it is better to think of services as augmenting it."[5]

BEING THERE FOR EACH OTHER

The term ICI served us well. But as the years passed and we had time to reflect on all we had experienced as part of the day-to-day life and maturation of Hope Meadows, we realized our community's primary purpose—to help children and their adoptive families—had undergone a change in character, reflecting David Brooks' writings on joy in his book, *The Road to Character*: "There's joy in a life filled with interdependence with others.... There's joy in freely chosen obedience to people, ideas, and commitments greater than oneself." He continues, "There's joy in that feeling of acceptance, the knowledge that though you don't deserve their love, others do love you; they have admitted you into their lives."[6]

The enduring, caring relationships of the neighbors gave form to Brooks' ideas, as did their commitment to Hope Meadows. From the beginning, every one of the adults said they wanted to be a part of Hope in order to "be there for the children." We had a vision of what this might look like, but no one, I believe, imagined how *interdependent* everyone would become, nor did we understand the importance of such reciprocal and mutually supportive, caring relationships—involving all generations—in addressing the ebb and flow of vulnerability. This was not intervention as it is usually understood.

At Hope, the children whom the seniors came to help would one day be helping them. And the parents, too, as their kids grew into teenagers, continued to rely on one another and on the special seniors in their life to advise, encourage, and be present. These same parents found themselves *being there* for the seniors—driving them to doctor's appointments, listening to their stories, and joining them to plan community activities such as the July 4th picnic and parade float. The seniors always tried to be there for the children, but almost from the start they also were there for each other as reflected in Joan's and Margie's stories.

We were still there to help the children—of course we were! But our community model had evolved from a one-way, directional commitment by adults to "vulnerable" children into a multidirectional commitment to *a way of life* where people of all ages, vulnerable or not, found joy in the security of mutual reliance, joy in participating in something "greater than oneself," and joy in knowing they were wanted, accepted and loved. Clearly that was true with Ben and Janice, with Al and Mr. Lee, with Joan and Alice, and with so many others.

FROM ICI TO INTENTIONAL NEIGHBORING

At one point, Tom Berkshire—chief of staff to the director of DCFS in our early years and a champion of our work—commented that Hope Meadows did not so much represent "community as intervention" as it did a new kind of intervention into the child welfare system!

Well, maybe. But more importantly we were seeing that our work wasn't about changing any one system; nor was it about services augmenting our strategy of community problem solving; it was about connecting people, creating relationships through neighboring where everyone was benefiting, not just the vulnerable group who were the initial focus of a community's purpose. Everyone—including those of us who rarely thought of ourselves as vulnerable—found our lives enriched. This was reflected in a description of Hope Meadows by the W.K. Kellogg Foundation: "As proximity and commitment combine to create love, all are hard pressed to determine which group [children, parents, or seniors] benefits the most."[7]

We realized our model of neighborhood intervention offered a way for all people involved to become *changemakers,* empowered as neighbors to contribute to the greater good by leveraging the power and natural dynamics of a small-scale, fully engaged community. Everyone was making a difference in not only helping to solve what seem at first to be insurmountable or overwhelming social problems (a commonly accepted idea of intervention), but, equally as important, by bringing back neighboring and reinventing community.

ICI no longer seemed to fit as a descriptive term. We began to refer to this community prototype not as an intervention through intergenerational community, but simply as *Intentional Neighboring*—wherein everyone was committed to and benefitted from a sense of shared purpose and belonging, friendships, and daily life filled with acts of thoughtfulness and compassion; where experiencing joy was a common occurrence.

Intentional neighboring is the term we use to this day, as it puts into action the belief that ordinary people of all ages and abilities as neighbors can be powerful assets in addressing the difficult challenges various vulnerable groups face. But it also encompasses an image of renewed hope, possibilities, and caring that reflects how all of us would like to think of ourselves and our communities. Imagine belonging to a community where:

- thoughtful neighbors come together to address some of our nation's most complex social challenges;
- those who are vulnerable are valued community members who participate and contribute; and,
- older adults find meaning and purpose in their daily lives, even at the end of life, through caring relationships and continuing engagement.

Sadly, for most, this vision of community is just that—a vision based on wishful thinking.

But at Hope Meadows, this was the reality—an evolving and never-perfect reality, but a reality nonetheless. One film producer, reading about Hope Meadows after the tragedy of the September

11 attacks, wrote to me: "As I read, I wept…for the vision, the lives that have been saved, the many that are still in need, and at a time when we need it most, a community model that…has its priorities in order. In terms of love, expansion, and peace Hope Meadows is a template for all to follow."[8]

Now, nearly two decades later, the concept of intentional neighboring is serving as a template for others to follow.

NEW LEADERS, NEW UNDERSTANDINGS

In working with change leaders[9] around the country who wanted to take our neighborhood intervention model and adapt it to a community they hoped to create, we found ourselves adapting our model in new locations not only for children who had been in foster care, but also for other vulnerable populations.

These inspiring leaders learned about us primarily from media stories and subsequent site visits. Initially, as expected, many of the inquiries came from people whose focus was on children from foster care. One of the first groups to work closely with us was *Bridge Meadows* in Portland, Oregon which became a community of nine family homes and twenty-seven elder apartments on two acres of land.[10] They focus on grandparents or other older relatives raising biological kin who had been in foster care. The elders have limited means, and all adults, including adoptive parents and legal guardians, are required to volunteer a minimum of 100 hours annually towards the benefit of the community.

Derenda Schubert, Bridge Meadows CEO, led efforts resulting in the opening of a second community nearby in Beaverton, Oregon in the fall of 2017. Both sites have limited staff and partner with off-site professionals throughout Portland. Over the years, as we have swapped stories, it has become clear that our core values remain solid. But we have also learned that design patterns vary as each site adapts to its place, people, and purpose. From Bridge Meadows we observed real differences, for example, between our rural and their urban setting and population, and between occupying two acres of land versus twenty.

Beyond the focus on foster care, we also received inquiries from many others who wanted to start an intentional intergenerational community for people with intellectual or developmental disabilities, single mothers and their children, returning veterans, struggling immigrant families, and people with dementia. The transformative leaders we began to work with believed passionately in our core values—these values were theirs too.

In recent years I have had the great pleasure in learning, not only from Bridge Meadows, but from three leaders whose interests did not revolve around foster care: Dylan Tête, who led the establishment of *Bastion: A Community of Resilience* in New Orleans for combat veterans and their families with lifelong rehabilitation needs; Karin Krause, who founded and operates *Hope & a Future* in Madison, Wisconsin for medically frail seniors and young at-risk families; and Deborah Finck, who is spearheading the effort to establish *Ohana Village* in Spokane, Washington as a community of practices addressing full inclusion for adults with developmental or intellectual disabilities. Like me, all have personal stories that strongly connect them to their work.

Dylan Tête

Dylan is a graduate of West Point and served combat duty in Iraq. He saw firsthand, and experienced himself, the wounds and causalities of war. Many of his veteran friends were slipping through the cracks because of the strong need for a community to combat social isolation. He decided he had to address this need and so began his journey to establish Bastion, an intentionally designed neighborhood in his native New Orleans for returning warriors and families, where the focus is on resilience and health through the development of meaningful intergenerational relationships that endure for a lifetime.

From our core values and design patterns, Dylan and his colleagues developed what they refer to as six core strategies: 1) an intentional environment, 2) community-based supports, 3) person-centered services, 4) professional partnerships, 5) property management, and 6) the promotion of positive health outcomes. Bastion utilizes professional services, but the primary intervention relies on seniors, to provide six hours per week of care and support to one another. Many of them are veterans themselves who bring with them empathy and understandings that provide powerful support for those who have recently returned from combat.

Dylan told me, "The trauma of war and loss reaches beyond the borders of Iraq and Afghanistan and into the homes of our military families. Sadly, Wounded Warriors and surviving families, especially children, must learn to cope and integrate into society." He went on to say, "The absence of community creates a dangerous void that can imperil and undermine the stability and on-going recovery of those impacted by trauma and loss."[11]

Karin Krause[12]

Karin grew up in a close-knit intergenerational community in a single-parent home, having lost her father when she was quite young. She knew the struggles single young mothers have to face, and she also knew how important relationships could be within a tight community. Her career began as a nurse working in institutional settings for very frail older adults. She quickly became disillusioned, and after one particularly hard day trying to comfort residents who were receiving inadequate care, she knew it was finally time for her to take some serious steps in providing a new kind of care for medically frail seniors.

Karin began by opening her home up to two of these seniors who—over time—made dramatic improvements in their physical and mental health. One came with severe dementia and the other with major physical health problems. She now has four medically frail seniors (all with dementia) living with her and her family in a spacious, renovated farmhouse on seven acres of land. These seniors receive professional-led, on-site care from people who, along with them, are part of one big caring family.

When I visited her not long ago, living in her home were also two adorable dogs that everyone seemed to love and a twenty-nine-year-old French chef who had a day job and, in exchange for reduced rent, cooked fabulous meals for the entire household most nights. Another resident was a young man—almost fifty—living with Down syndrome. His mother, who also lived there, suffered from dementia. She died just months before my visit. How wonderful to see him be able to go on with his life, remaining in a familiar and loving home where he was happy, valued, and surrounded by people he cared about and who cared about him.

Karin is now in the process of building owner-occupied condominium units for active seniors (aged 55+), co-located with new affordable rental housing units for at-risk families with young children. In this intentional intergenerational community, through shared experiences and regular contact, she believes everyone—medically frail seniors, active seniors, young at-risk families, and staff—will benefit from helping as much as from being helped. Also benefiting is the broader Madison community, from which Karin draws over three hundred people regularly as volunteers, including a chaplain, musicians, carpenters, techies, and gardeners.

Deborah Finck

Deb and her husband Charlie adopted their son Jonathan as a newborn. He was conceived in the institution where his birth mother lived most of her life, and at age twenty-six he is a highly social and artistic young man. He also lives with profound autism. Deb knew that one day soon she and Charlie would no longer be able to care adequately for Jonathan in their home. They also knew he needed, like all of us, a place where he belonged and could thrive, and for that to happen a new kind of community response was necessary. When Deb learned about Hope Meadows, she saw a living example of what was needed—not only for Jonathan, but for so many of the millions of individuals who are living with intellectual and developmental disabilities. She writes:

> In theory, community-based residential opportunities increase independence and access. But real engagement within communities is not accomplished by location alone. Our ability to thrive always depends upon the relationships we build and the extent to which we can participate in and contribute to the lives of others. To become truly inclusive, communities must change, and be supported in those changes toward a readiness to embrace the mutual benefits and responsibilities of living with one another. An integrated, intentional community of support is a model for and commitment to that change.[13]

Being a Little Crazy Helps

Strong leaders of intentional communities based on caring for and supporting neighbors must be optimists, risk takers—and a little crazy. As such, I think we have a strong tendency to think big (and I hope realistically), knowing that the people we are building our communities around—returning warriors, medically frail seniors, at-risk young families, and children who have experienced foster care—all face many challenges. Their challenges are consistent with those faced by Americans with developmental disabilities through the life course, and they point directly to the circumstances impacting all but the most fortunate of us at various times in our lives. Building Ohana publishes this list of challenges on their website:

- Housing shortages
- Rising cost of care
- Discrimination
- Fragmented service systems
- Broken families
- Isolation and loneliness
- Unemployment
- Food insecurity
- Chronic neglect
- Aging alone
- Immobility
- Poverty
- Segregation[14]

I would add to this list an almost overwhelming sense of dependency and powerlessness.

Change leaders like Derenda, Dylan, Karin, and Deb, along with others doing similar work are just crazy enough to believe that over time their communities—through intentional neighboring—will be able to address and lessen the negative impact of many of the challenges listed above. In doing so, all of us including the most vulnerable among us will live lives of hope and thanksgiving. And in doing so, through caring relationships with each other our communities will serve as a model of civil society at its very best and at a time when we truly need it most.

- Twelve -

Design Patterns to Strengthen Social Connection

> Caring can be learned by all human beings, can be worked into the design of every life, meeting an individual need as well as a pervasive need in society.[1]
>
> —Mary Catherine Bateson, *Composing a Life*

STEPPING BACK AND LOOKING DEEPER

As my colleagues and I worked with change leaders and became better at articulating what intentional neighboring is and why it is so important, we knew there was more we still needed to do. The work of Christopher Alexander, author and highly acclaimed architect and design theorist, encouraged us to believe that the power to make a neighborhood come alive is firmly rooted in each of us. Influenced by his work, the question we kept asking ourselves was, "What is it besides our three foundational values that is needed in order to tap this power, to make intentional neighboring real, to make it come alive?" We began by identifying operational principles that had served us well at Hope Meadows. Eventually we realized we were describing *design patterns,* a term coined by Alexander in *The Timeless Way of Building*.

Design patterns are broad guidelines that can be implemented in various and often innovative ways, and they are much like seeds in that they have different results when planted in different soil. Alexander explains that design patterns must adapt to the "natural and unpredictable changes that inevitably arise in the life of a community."[2] For our work, these patterns were essential. As David Hopping observed, "Together they form an intuitive template for creating opportunities and supports for successful interaction and long-term flourishing, and when implemented flexibly and creatively, can resolve the natural tensions entailed in forming community out of diversity."[3]

A decade later, four key design patterns remain salient as other nonprofits, inspired by Hope Meadows, have incorporated them as part of their operational guidelines. These include first, an intentional focus on vulnerability; second, three or more generations living as neighbors; third, the physical designing of the neighborhood to strengthen relationships; and fourth, the embracing of diversity. Each of these design patterns is intended, as Alexander argues, "*to change what would happen in their absence.*"[4] Each is critically important in bringing people with a shared purpose together, and in creating a community where caring and kindness proliferate—where people come alive.

INTENTIONAL FOCUS ON VULNERABILITY

Design Pattern One: *The organizational focus of the community is on a particular population experiencing complex and specific* *challenges that make them vulnerable and in need of support.*

In communities based on intentional neighboring, the specific focus on families and individuals facing persistent challenges is at the heart of the community's purpose. Vulnerable people frequently experience sustained forms of disadvantage, hardship, and loneliness; the result can be life-long adverse consequences that threaten their wellbeing and lead to high psychosocial and economic costs. All need a safe, secure, inclusive environment, with neighbors they know—people who understand them, care about them, and provide them support. They also need opportunities to assume their indispensable roles in the lives of others. Such populations may include people with developmental disabilities; children and youth in foster care or aging out of foster care; people at the end of life; homeless LGBTQ youth; parents and youth returning from incarceration; returning soldiers; and poor working families, to name a few.

The intentional focus on a vulnerable population and its full inclusion into community is essential. As a source of identity and community cohesion, it helps to unite people regardless of their differences. At Hope Meadows, the focus was on children in foster care who needed adoptive homes. People moved to Hope Meadows to "be there for the children;" in doing so, seniors realized they needed to be there for the parents as well, and the parents soon came to understand that they needed to be there for the seniors. But always they said they were there for the children. Effie King put it this way:

> I think the reason people become close here is because of the love for the children and the caring for one another and what we are all trying to do—the seniors caring for the families and what they are trying to do with the

> children, and the families caring for the seniors because they know we are trying to help them in any and every way we can.... Everyone believes in the Hope program, and that is why we are living here. You have to love the children and what everybody is trying to do for the children. If you don't have that, you are in the wrong place.[5]

Just as our values represent critical differences from common perceptions and practices, so do our design patterns. Hope's unifying vision around a particular population identified as vulnerable created a community nothing like the typical neighborhood we now see in America. And although Hope was indeed an *intentional community*, we differed from those whose intention it was to create any kind of substantially *alternative lifestyle.* We were not experimenting with solar power, living off the grid, or growing our own organic food. Instead, we strived, as I have stated previously, to achieve "normal" community life—something many children in foster care had never experienced. We wanted a neighborhood where everyone, but especially the children, would feel a sense of safety, permanency, and connection. We encouraged neighboring at its very best—a kind of ideal version of normal—something our Hope team playfully referred to as *designer normality.*

THREE OR MORE GENERATIONS AS NEIGHBORS

Design Pattern Two: *Housing developments and neighborhoods are designed to include residents spanning three or more generations.*

We recognized that the energy, care, and resilience brought to people's lives by three or more generations are necessary for a community to thrive, for everyone to benefit. Complex interactions and relationships developing among three or more generations give rise to a more robust culture of neighboring and a deeper understanding and appreciation of the unique perspectives of each generation. At Hope Meadows, children brought joy, meaning, and purpose to the daily life of older adults; parents delighted in older adults becoming their friends, mentors, and "grandparents" to their children; and older adults took pride in making themselves available to provide care and support to parents, to their children, and to one another.

Debbie Calhoun, one of the first parents to move to Hope, in a video produced by the W. K. Kellogg Foundation said: "It is like we are all one big family. They talk about the seniors being grandparents for the kids, but they have filled a void in my life. They not only help the kids; they are here for all of us."

In this same piece, Debbie's daughter, an incredibly sensitive and aware teen, described Hope this way:

> Here there's an automatic sense of looking out for each other, so in that case, the seniors benefit. And then, I think about the kids who came here who need more than one-on-one in school attention, so of course the kids benefit. But then I think of the parents too and the things they are learning about their own capacity as far as loving, learning how to be patient.[6]

To include three or more generations as a design pattern is quite atypical. Rarely is the importance of three or more generations emphasized by programs that focus on uniting generations or on "intergenerational programming." Much more typical are two-generation program models with the generations being children and older adults. This has become such common practice that when one is talking about "intergenerational" or even "multigenerational" interactions, relationships, or programs, it is almost always assumed these words refer to just two generations. Even in the media articles about Hope Meadows, there has often been a primary focus on relationships between the seniors and the kids, rather than between kids, parents and seniors.

Thoughtful planning is required to encourage three or more generations to be actively engaged as neighbors. The fruits of such planning in our case included incorporating specific physical design as outlined below, as well as involving all generations in the majority of community activities and designing policies to encourage the interaction and development of neighboring among residents of all ages.

PHYSICAL DESIGN FACILITATES RELATIONSHIPS

Design Pattern Three: *The physical design dimensions of a community are vital as a context for the formation and development of caring relationships across and within generations, and among a diverse population.*

Christopher Alexander's work is notable for promoting architectural practices that put people at the heart of the design process. He argues that for a community to flourish, the design process must include not only the traditional bricks and mortar aspects of buildings and neighborhoods, but the creation of an environment that nurtures human life and is designed by the people and for the people.[7] Traditional practices, as I have said, take a long time to change, and today it remains in typical housing development that it is not the nurturing of people but the cost-to-build, price points and marketability of homes and units that are the dominant considerations of design. Amenities, such as community gardens, walking paths and playgrounds might be included for the pleasures they offer to residents, but their value is marketed on the basis of *what we do in those places* rather than on the community relationships they might foster. Little thought is given to the impact of physical design and built environment on the social and psychological dimensions of neighborhoods. Our cultural predilection for privacy is the one notable exception to that rule.

In his recently published *Palaces for the People*, Eric Klinenberg focuses on the profound importance of the design component, *social infrastructure*, defined as "the physical conditions that determine whether social relationships develop." Klinenberg believes that for neighborhoods to flourish, social infrastructure must be robust and purposeful, intent on fostering "contact, mutual support, and collaboration among friends and neighbors."[8]

The lessons in community building we learned at Hope helped us to understand firsthand the importance of design and social infrastructure. In considering replication, we always emphasized two essential points: buildings and outdoor spaces should be designed so all generations could easily comingle, and they should be designed for accessible aging in place within community. These insights, while becoming universally accepted in today's world, were relatively new when we first began working with architects. At that time there had been little research to draw upon in designing communities and homes to facilitate multigenerational living. One architect we met who was working on a plan for a potential replication site had never designed a community for active intergenerational living. His early drawings situated housing for seniors at one end of the piece of property and housing for families at the opposite end. In the middle he put a community center and a playground.

This design clearly did not reflect the intergenerational dynamics that had come to exist at Hope Meadows. and for that reason I was a bit flabbergasted to see such a plan. In my usual well-meaning but not-so-subtle way, I blurted, "This is simply not acceptable!" Thank goodness David Hopping was with me. Brilliant, thoughtful, and soft spoken, he stepped in to orchestrate the conversation and I stepped aside. It was not long before the architect had his aha moment and began reworking the design, eventually coming up with a wonderfully innovative plan for blending housing to foster intergenerational relationships.

Good design must also consider the needs we all have as we face our last years, helping us to remain in and be a part of our community. As we lose health and mobility, and when there is a lack of safe, appropriate, and accessible housing, a vital link in the *circle of care*[9] is broken; older adults become isolated and our children are denied opportunities to learn about compassion, reciprocity, and interdependence, to understand that people facing old age matter. A community's failure to meet the housing needs of seniors, especially older seniors, teaches children that some community members are expendable and that we are obliged to care for others only when it is easy to do so.

Finally, the ideal community has both outdoor and indoor space designed to meet the needs of all generations. Intergenerational outdoor gathering spots are usually playgrounds and picnic areas where people of all ages can gather to play games, hold celebrations, or just be there for each other—just as Joe Stang was there for Keith when he was tagged out and left the playground in tears, or when seniors would stand guard after school as two or three kids gathered to play. Not too long after Hope began, we created a memorial garden (with funding support from Oprah Winfrey), a quiet place to sit alone or with friends, and a gathering place to honor Hope residents who had died. On Memorial Day we often replaced a brick in the garden patio with one engraved with the name of someone who had died. During these events, children raised the flag on the flagpole, parents or seniors read poems or stories, and often all three generations came together to sing a song. Kids and parents pushed people in wheelchairs across the expansive grass to the garden because we didn't have paved paths—one more thing to add to our "to do" list.

To our surprise, another popular outdoor gathering space actually came with the military housing: the carport! None of our homes were designed with porches. At first, we were disappointed, knowing the value of the front porch in fostering neighboring relationships. We wondered how we'd do without them. But soon we saw that the carports functioned in their place, and even had certain advantages; they became spacious gathering places at ground level, easily accessible to everyone, from kids on bikes to anyone using wheelchairs or walkers. No one had to maneuver steps.

Sitting in the carport became an open invitation for others to come up and visit. Mr. Lee sat in his every morning, weather permitting, watching and talking to the children on their way to school. One mother described a typical interaction:

> Both my boys…every morning, they go out and the first thing they do is look for Mr. Lee. And they'd do this man thing, hollering up the street: 'Hey there, Mr. Lee!'
> 'What are you doing, kids?'
> 'Getting ready to go to school," they'd yell back to him.
> 'You be good to your mama. You listen to your mama.'
> 'Okay, Mr. Lee, we will!'[10]

Other seniors waited in their carports as school let out, just waiting for the children to stop by to talk. And on warm summer evenings neighbors gathered regularly in a resident's carport and driveway, just to socialize and have a good time.

Hope Meadows had plenty of land for the creation of outdoor gathering spots for the residents, but the military housing ultimately used to create Hope Meadows did not include adequate space for large indoor gatherings. While the original placement and orientation of the houses worked well to foster relationships quickly between families who were often stationed at the base for only a short period of time, we had no building in our neighborhood with room enough to accommodate all 100 or more residents at one time for celebrations or community meetings. During the summer holidays we gathered on the playground, but in winter we had to leave Hope and meet in a hall in the larger community of Rantoul. Our seniors insisted on a community center, and soon we converted two of our duplex housing units into our very own gathering spot, named by the community as the "Intergenerational Center" or IGC for short. Creating this center was one of the best design decisions we ever made.

At one time over thirty activities were held there weekly. In the early morning, seniors gathered for coffee and yes, gossip; during the day parents and seniors might meet for an exercise class or a lesson on financial planning provided by an invited speaker. After school, kids were tutored in rooms that had once been bedrooms, or they engaged with seniors in the library or computer room. In the great room we served snacks, set up board games, and implemented special projects for kids, seniors and staff. Every month parents and seniors hosted Girl Scout meetings, movie nights, special meetings, and community potlucks.

I have heard that neighborhood community centers are empty much of the time. At Hope Meadows, just the opposite was true. It was filled with people throughout the day and often into the evening, serving as the heart of the community, bringing all generations together.

Other design features in Hope enhanced community engagement. All homes were oriented to the life of the community, and extra-large windows in the living rooms provided significant visual connection to the outdoors. When anyone walked or drove by, people in their homes could see them. Hope neighbors had almost exclusive use of our streets, and if they saw someone outside, they would often stop in their cars and chat. If a resident was sick, a recliner or hospital bed could be moved to anyone's living room to keep that person connected to the life of the neighborhood. Hope was also blessed with lots of green space, visible from every home, a feature which research is now showing is very beneficial to mental health.

We could not have known when we began our journey all of the different ways people would connect due to the social infrastructure of Hope Meadows. This is in part because, as Klinenberg writes in quoting sociologist Susan Leigh Star, infrastructure is invisible, "part of the background for other kinds of work."[11] We simply took for granted the IGC, the memorial garden, car ports, and our playground as added amenities to our housing—public settings where people gathered to interact with friends and neighbors.

As time passed, due to the age of our housing when we purchased it and to the *constant* use of our public settings by our residents, something always needed to be replaced—a toilet, carpeting in the IGC, woodchips under playground equipment—or repaired—cracked sidewalks, furnaces, plumbing, and the like. To maintain these unglamourous but essential features of our neighborhood required that we budget our time and financial resources. As Klinenberg astutely observes, social infrastructure "becomes most visible when it breaks down." When social infrastructure is neglected, he writes, "it inhibits social activity, leaving families and individuals to fend for themselves."[12] Given a choice, most of us tend to spend less time in parks and playgrounds overgrown with weeds or in rundown, inaccessible gathering spaces in favor of more time in our private homes where we are safe and comfortable, even if we are alone. At Hope, that tendency would have run counter to our purposes. For us it had to be a daily priority to make sure our shared and public spaces were well kept, visually pleasing and inviting—inside and out—to draw our residents together and to reflect the esteem we had for each and every one of them, even when it sometimes strained our resources.

EMBRACING DIVERSITY

Design Pattern Four: *Diversity is valued as a way to generate creative solutions to complex problems while reducing stigma, stereotypes, and intolerance.*

As with so much else of importance about Hope Meadows, diversity wasn't something we artfully planned from the beginning. It simply happened that the inherent diversity of age was accompanied by the diversity of the parents and seniors in relation to race, ethnicity, education, income, and life experience and perspective. The children who came to us from the foster care system were more homogeneous except for race. At any given time, seventy-plus percent were black and twenty to twenty-five percent were white. Only one child was Hispanic. This racial breakdown was similar for the children who came with their biological parents.

As our first group of residents moved into Hope Meadows, it was racial diversity that caused many to be wary, nervous and concerned. Most of them had no previous connections to people of different races, and this was particularly true for our seniors and children. It was not as true for the middle generation of parents, most of whom had lived a much more integrated life.

We saw first-hand that when diverse people live next door to each other or down the street, when they connect every day, and when they *share a common purpose*, the significance of their differences tends to evaporate. This occurs over time and as people come to know and to rely on one another for support and friendship. Stereotypes and prejudices that individuals may have carried throughout their lives begin to disappear as open and honest communication, reciprocal acts of care, and growing understandings become routine, a part of everyday life.

These transformations at Hope were happily unlegislated and mostly accomplished by simple yet powerful acts. A child, for example, helps a senior carry in groceries. In return, the senior gives the child a hug, and the child rewards the senior with a grateful, delighted smile. Both give and get what each person needs. Or seniors of different races live next door to each other and discover they share a love of gardening. Soon, they are sharing seeds, planting and pulling weeds together. By the time they are ready to reap the harvest of vegetables and flowers, these two seniors are sharing not only gardening but produce, family details, and life histories. Trust grows, and eventually they watch one another's apartment and collect mail when the other goes out of town. Racial difference becomes inconsequential as their daily lives merge.

Miss Irene, like many of the seniors who had lived their entire lives in small, white, rural communities, would tell me she'd never touched the skin of a black person until moving to Hope Meadows. Now she was in love with her Hope grandchildren, most of whom were black. One fall, she told the following story about taking Leon to visit her brother's farm, located in an all-white community.

> I learned that Leon didn't know what a tractor was and asked my brother if I could bring him up just to ride the tractor. On the way up, it brought tears to my eyes when the little, bitty boy [age 6] put his hand on my arm and asked, 'Grandma, do they know I'm black?' He was just kind of leery about it, how they were going to accept him because his skin was different.
>
> I said, 'Well Grandma's skin's different too. Is that all right with you?'
>
> 'Oh yeah.' he says.
>
> When we got there, the nephews were all fine with this. They saw Leon, and one of my nephews picked him up and said, 'Come on, we've got work to do.' And they ... put him in that pick-up truck and his little head was bobbing back and forth across the field. It was beautiful, it really was, and Leon's eyes were like dollars. And they got him on a combine, and on a corn picker. He sat on Grandpa's lap, and he was driving that corn picker. And then the little boy talked on the CB...he did everything.
>
> Before he left the field, he ran over to my brother, hugged him all on his own and said, 'Thanks Grandpa!'
>
> My brother walked back to our truck wiping his eyes, and he said, 'That's some lad. That dear little boy, he's a sweetheart I'll tell you.'
>
> On the way home, I told Leon that we would get fried chicken. He put his little hand on my arm and said, 'Let's not get fried chicken; it's too expensive. Let's just get a

hamburger.' So we did. Then while we were eating, he got pretty serious; he said he wished he had a grandpa like that.

'Little man, I said, 'I think you've got one.'[13]

A trip to the farm during the fall harvest became an annual event for Miss Irene and Leon. When Leon learned to read, his one wish was for Miss Irene to take him to the farm so he could read to her relatives—which he did. Miss Irene often lamented, "There's only one thing that I regret at this stage in my life, and that's that I won't be around to watch him when he grows up." Not only did Miss Irene and Leon soon learn to look beyond race, so did their family members living in the broader community.

Ironically, there were instances in our early years when racially-based acts by the broader community calculated to exacerbate racial fears and strife within Hope Meadows resulted in just the opposite—bringing us together. One morning, I arrived at my office in the neighborhood to find by the front door a black rag doll with a noose around its neck. On another occasion, one of our interracial families woke to find nails spilled all over their driveway. We never learned who the perpetrators of these acts were. We did learn something about ourselves: these acts of race-based intimidation made us all the more determined to carry out Hope's mission. We were there for the children who needed us and whom we needed. We would be there for one another.

Diversity is a popular word, but the environments we create often cultivate sameness and uniformity. This is especially evident in housing developments, institutional settings, and neighborhoods where it is common to find people segregated by age, race, income, *etc.* Some examples are whole communities designed for active, mature adults, group homes for people who have disabilities, assisted living facilities, and low-income housing projects.

We know that segregation only reinforces harmful stigmas and stereotypes, but many of us live that way, unconsciously feeding our discomfort about proximity and intimacy with those who are different than us. Studies reveal that we all carry unconscious biases and prejudices; in 2007, American sociologist Robert Putnam published research suggesting that "too much diversity" can actually lead to social retreat and thus can be harmful to civic life.[14] I don't dispute that this may indeed happen, but it certainly doesn't have to happen. Because we had strong values and intentions around relationships at Hope, retreat was not an option. Instead, we watched ourselves grow closer as ignorance was replaced with understanding, fear with comfort, and apathy with care and concern. Living in a community designed to embrace and incorporate differences was not always easy, but the benefits far outweighed and for the most part overcame any tensions and conflicts. We realized that our success was in no small measure because of—not in spite of—our differences.

Diversity—simply defined as the presence of differences within a particular environment—is really only bad or good to the extent that it advances health and resilience. Deb Finck is a tireless advocate for inclusion, and she writes, "In nature, a diverse landscape is inherently stronger, resistant to natural disasters. In society, diversity requires *inclusion* in order to contribute added strength and value—a kind of cultural invitation to invite all people, no matter our age, ability, race or income, to engage and contribute, and a collective willingness to RSVP to that invitation."[15] The creation of Hope Meadows brought a diverse population together, but our mutual values and purposes created *inclusion*.

We implemented practices and policies to reinforce the value of diversity and inclusion, beginning with the *expectation* (included in our housing and employment contracts with seniors and parents) that everyone was to contribute to the betterment of the community through engagement as a neighbor and as a community member. We *embraced and celebrated activities* that brought us together and actually showcased our residents' diverse backgrounds and experiences. Our intergenerational trips, both local and national, helped us expand relationships with one another and our world. Activities such as our monthly reading night—suggested by a retired reading teacher—brought residents of all ages together to read to one another. Every room in our community center—and all of our shared spaces (with the exception of a children's therapy room)—were open to everyone, young and old. There were no "adults only" spaces.

At Hope Meadows there was no easy way of retreating from one another. Our intentional commitment to embrace diversity continued to foster surprising and highly creative ideas—we never knew what the next plan to bring us together might be. Sharing and valuing ideas for helping one another, working and playing with the children together and laughing together all reinforced the value of diversity as a way to generate creative solutions to complex problems and reduce stigma, stereotypes, and intolerance.

Key components of the Hope Meadows experience—expecting residents to engage in the community; making this expectation part of our legal contracts; embracing and celebrating special activities and annual events; creating inclusive, all-community shared spaces, and, perhaps most importantly, sharing our Hope purposes—reminded residents to take leadership in creating and modeling commitment, caring, and respect for all. We reflected the conclusion of Andrew Solomon, that "Intimacy with difference fosters its accommodation," and through this process we expand "definitions of the human family."[16] Solomon was referring to parents and their children who were deeply troubled or had a disability. Clearly the individual families at Hope could relate, but key components of the Hope Meadows experience fostered the accommodation of difference for the entire community, not just individual families.

IMPLEMENTING DESIGN PATTERNS

It's easy to talk about our design patterns—intentionally focusing on a vulnerable population, integrating three or more generations, designing for maximum social interaction, and deliberately incorporating diversity into community planning. But implementation is hard work! It took me a long time to realize that each component represents a *critical difference* from "conventional" practice. No wonder it often felt that—even though what we were doing was based on research, common sense, and basic values of compassion and kindness—there always seemed to be resistance to what we practiced and what we preached, especially by child welfare professionals and the court system.

This was because Hope's values and beliefs diverged from common understandings and assumptions that guide current practices and policies. Our programs defied prevailing logic and ways of operating. Once commonly accepted views and practices become ingrained ways of thinking and those practices become codified within long-standing institutions, *change is hard and happens slowly*. But change did happen at Hope Meadows. Our mission to address the need of children in foster care for a permanent, nurturing family and a safe and caring community was compelling. In time, through the implementation of design patterns and guided by core values, a new model of child welfare intervention and of community living emerged.

STAFF MATTERS

Just as we, to be successful at intervention and community cohesion, had to rethink how we viewed family, vulnerability, and older adults, we also had to view the purpose and role of professional staff through a new lens. It might be natural to conclude that paid professional staff are not necessary or even relevant as Hope's residents embrace their roles as caring neighbors and staff recede into the background. This conclusion would be wrong.

At Hope Meadows, on-site professionals, including our therapist, social worker, family advocate, and activity coordinator, continually engaged in the crucial work of supporting and encouraging residents to use their talents, experiences, and interests to build and maintain a strong community, one built on caring connections. This work was ongoing as our resident population grew, evolved, and aged. As staff we were always adapting our work to new and changing circumstances that required we constantly communicate and demonstrate our core values and the importance of our design patterns. Without this leadership, as Kruzes and Posner observe in their book, *The Leadership Challenge*, "...constituents have no energizer to ignite their passion, no example to follow, no compass by which to be guided."[17]

To be successful in empowering community members to promote the wellbeing of one another, Hope staff worked in inconspicuous ways. A parent, for example, might casually mention to the family advocate how much she would love to be able to provide piano lessons for one of her kids. Instead of making arrangements for Miss Carol or Mr. Bob—both pianists—to provide these lessons, we encouraged the mother to ask them directly if they might teach her child as part of their volunteer work. This strategy worked out well, and neither the parent nor the seniors needed us to manage the process or to work out the details; our job was simply to jumpstart dialogue between the residents.

For residents to feel comfortable coming to us with requests or concerns, we first had to build trusting relationships through listening, hearing concerns, and then offering suggestions for what the residents themselves might or could do to address the concerns. When needed and when we could, we found space or provided materials or small amounts of money so that what a resident wanted to do could be accomplished. Maybe we would reimburse them for meat for a community picnic they were planning or rent a space in the broader community so everyone could attend a special event. Often, we provided supplies for afterschool activities or an honorarium for a special speaker.

DAILY RELATIONSHIPS WITH SUPPORT PROFESSIONALS

Our Hope staff were indeed professionals, all with college degrees and training in their fields. What was unique about their work were the on-the-ground, intentional encounters with residents as we lived daily life together. Whereas most people work with professionals on an occasional basis, by appointment and very often in clinical surroundings, our staff experienced daily life with the children, parents and seniors in our community. I believe this enabled us to build trust and inspire one another in our mutual mission. The residents knew that staff were there to support them. Our therapist was always available to see children and parents—not only in the therapeutic playroom, but on the playground and sidewalks, in the IGC, and in family homes. Every day, our activity coordinator worked side-by-side with volunteers in the afterschool program making sure that there were planned activities and materials to carry out the activities. She also served as a security blanket for volunteers making tough decisions such as whether or not to enforce rules regarding acceptable behavior (e.g., no running or hitting) when they did not want to take on this responsibility.

RELATIONAL LEADERSHIP

Staff were always around to offer praise, guidance, encouragement, support, and friendship. They were also always available to help educate residents about the effects of trauma on children's development and behavior, and to help them in their journey to understand the meaning and implications of our core values and design patterns. These were not just one-time teachings, but recurring conversations and ongoing learning opportunities, often had over coffee or in the context of a particular circumstance. We all worked hard to help residents cast aside common and deeply-held beliefs that place undue burdens on individuals and families and diminish the worth of people. Our challenge was to transform these beliefs in favor of a collective and interdependent community response to human needs, recognizing the power of caring relationships and the value of every individual in our midst. Our responsibility was to always do this with respect for the dignity of every resident and the tremendous value of their contributions. Our jobs were a kind of servant leadership—we were there to help a community of people be there for one another, as Margie and Joan both said, "to do for each other."

Scholars Lone Hersted and Kenneth J. Gergen would have

called our form of leadership *relational leading*[18]—a relational process where we, following the work of sociologist Laurel Richardson, "walked with" the members of the neighborhood. In 'walking with,' we were not 'insiders' or 'outsiders.'[19] Rather we were partial knowers and conveners working together toward a common purpose, within a special place, and with a like-minded group of people. We did, however, as Hersted and Gergen write, have a heightened responsibility, serving as a model for the residents and, as illustrated above, "setting in motion the kinds of relational practices most needed." As such we taught and "invited forms of interchange from which the organization [was] nourished and from which new potentials [were] created."[20]

These practices often took what Sharon Allen, a highly respected leader in the Champaign-Urbana community, refers to as "ordinary courage," which she defines as "the decision to stand, often in the smallest of ways, for things that align with your core, and taking action when others can't or more often, won't." When community and courage intersect, Sharon believes, "the result is power and inspiration."[21]

I came to realize it was not always easy for staff to be a part of this new intentional neighboring/relational leadership strategy. It was not how they had been trained, nor was it intuitive. As David Hopping observed, "From a professional staff perspective, it's a challenge to cultivate and work with this kind of organizational capacity because it's so indirect—sort of like trying to back double semi-trailers into a parking lot. Not everyone is up to it."[22]

THE BIG BOSS

To say I am no computer whiz is an understatement, so it was to everyone's surprise when I started reading Tom DeMarco and

Timothy Lister's writings about successful software team development. Their insight on managers spoke to me as the executive director of the nonprofit responsible for the success of Hope Meadows. They wrote:

> ...good managers provide frequent easy opportunities for the team to succeed together.... The best success is the one in which there is no evident management, in which the team works as a genial aggregation of peers. The best boss is the one who can manage this over and over again without the team members knowing they've been "managed."[23]

Attending one of our Hope summer picnics, Wayland overheard two young boys talking about the event. "It's Brenda's birthday" one said.

"Who's Brenda?" his friend asked.

"She is the BIG boss." he replied, causing my husband to smile at that idea ever since.

As "the big boss," managing a diverse team of staff and community members, my job was to facilitate collaborative, reciprocal, trusting, friendly, and supportive relationships among all of us. When I was successful—and there were definitely times when I was not—"managing" took on a very different meaning. I tried to help residents and staff alike to understand and accept the reality that our words, our decisions, and our behaviors in regard to Hope relationships were often departures from what was normal, familiar, or even comfortable. While continually trying to instill our core values, I worked to encourage and empower all involved with Hope Meadows to remain open and flexible to the needs of the community as it continued to evolve.

Together, as a "genial aggregate of peers," we tried not to take ourselves too seriously, frequently laughing at ourselves and with each other. But make no mistake in thinking our work was trivial or easy. While we experienced an overall sense of communal joy and friendship, we were ever aware of the serious and important work of our mission: to be there for and to ensure the wellbeing of one another, especially the most vulnerable. This task we took very, very seriously.

- Thirteen -

I'm Coming Over and I'm Bringing my Suitcase

'There is no use trying,' said Alice; 'One can't believe impossible things.'

'I dare say you haven't had much practice,' said the Queen. 'When I was your age, I always did it for half an hour a day. Why, sometimes I've believed as many as six impossible things before breakfast.'[1]

—Lewis Carroll, *Through the Looking Glass*

A COUNTRY DIVIDED

Some say that we are a fractured nation, fractured beyond repair. Instead of coming together to address social problems, Americans seem—almost by the day—to be increasingly divided. The need for resources is pitting advocates for the old against those for the young; allegations of discrimination and different points of view daily separate people based on age and race, immigration status, religion, political affiliations, gender, ability, and wealth.

And now, perhaps more than ever in our history, our youth are at risk. High school students today cannot remember a time when there was little or no threat of gun violence in our schools or when we were not at war. David Brooks recently described the young undergraduate and graduate students currently enrolled in our nation's colleges as "a generation emerging from the wreckage." He writes for *The New York Times* that they do not trust in our institutions or in America as a land they can be proud of. More than anything, Brooks concludes, this generation hungers for an environment characterized by "social and emotional bonding"—for positive relationships.[2]

They are not alone. We all yearn for a sense of shared citizenship, an overarching bond that reflects common purposes, a common humanity. But evidence of this bond is scant. Our divisions are deep, sometimes even deadly, and the idea that we might join together to address the challenges affecting us all has begun to feel like a pipe dream—an impossibility.

Yet for years I experienced the coming *alongside and standing with one another* of people who were deeply different from one another, including those perceived to be most vulnerable. At Hope, people of different races, ages, and political persuasions became close friends bound together all the more by the common purposes they shared. Their heartfelt daily relationships offered that "social and emotional bonding" out of which love, joy, and gratitude emerged. Like senior Jim Saunders, we all felt "a little emotional at times…to see the changes in the children…," and indeed in all of us. Because we are always changed by deep and meaningful connection to one another, in families, in neighborhoods, and in cities and countries as well, we need—now more than ever—to be able to trust in the strength and resilience of these connections no matter how different we might be.

As new communities of intentional neighboring emerge, committed neighbors, including some of our most underserved and disenfranchised individuals, are contributing to this unifying work. John, a veteran diagnosed with PTSD, depression, and anxiety disorder, was living in his car and couch surfing at the home of friends. After returning home from the Middle East, nothing made sense to him. He needed help, but he also needed a new sense of purpose, and no part of our traditional social safety net was helping him to reconnect with life back home. For the last year, John has lived in Bastion's Community of Resilience, surrounded by neighbors and staff who understand him. He explains it this way: "Now, I feel I have a responsibility to other people, my neighbors, whose hearts are in the community as much as mine. It feels nice to be needed again and know that I can help. I feel like Bastion is pushing the boundaries, and I'm part of that too."[3]

John's neighbors are as diverse as those at Hope Meadows, and like Hope Meadows, it is Bastion's purpose that unites its residents. These communities are not fractured; here, everyone works for the greater good; here, everyone benefits from participating in the creation of a culture of care, kindness and compassion. But the question remains: how do we transform the life-giving lifestyle of a few planned and purposeful neighborhoods into a way of living for all of us? Is this even possible?

"A BEACON OF POSSIBILITY IN A WORLD IN NEED OF HOPE"

When first the idea and then the reality of Hope Meadows began to take over my life twenty-five plus years ago, my friends and colleagues feared I was wasting my time. The project was too big, too radical and idealistic, too ambitious, and far too risky. After all, we were bringing together, as *Nightline's* Ted Koppel quipped, "a whole bundle of problems." On a then empty military base, we were combining seniors, mostly retired, some with health issues, and many with nothing to do; overworked, frustrated and under-supported foster families; and, up to forty children wounded by egregious abuse and neglect. We were at once a licensed foster care/adoption agency (state), a family neighborhood (private), a social service center (nonprofit), and a housing project (market). What made me think this would work?

Who would move there? Did we truly believe people would adopt these highly troubled kids? Where would we find staff and the money to pay them? And while we obtained housing for a song, who could replicate that? How would any nonprofit be able to raise enough money to obtain land and build homes? (This last question has always been initially the toughest to address, and it has caused many projects to remain just someone's dream.) But we did find answers, and they continue to emerge. Ted Koppel said that by putting together a whole bundle of problems we "appeared to have produced a whole bunch of solutions."[4] Talk about the impossible!

Often in my life the impossible has become possible, the unlikely has been made true. I did fight the Pentagon and win—with a lot of help, to be sure. Kenny did learn to read against all odds, and then grew up to share the joy of books with his beloved Grandpa Al; Elsa is still listening to the music of her family symphony. Two of her kids graduated from well-regarded universities, she is grandmother to two beautiful children who live near her, and she works at a job she loves. Steve lived the last ten years of his life at Hope Meadows in full giving mode, despite a series of debilitating strokes. Afflicted over and over again, he nonetheless insisted these were the best years of his life. And Miss Irene, whose only regret was that she would never live long enough to see her beloved Hope grandchildren grow up—well, she saw it all. Now, as I write, I am mourning her passing. She died one week ago, just two weeks shy of her ninety-fourth birthday. Her dear Leon, now thirty, stayed in touch with her, even surprising her with a visit after his move to Rhode Island.

And so I have come to believe that *we can change things*—no outcome is etched in stone. Some believe that when the impossible becomes a reality, it is a miracle. I am more pragmatic, knowing the implementation of new ideas is mostly a slow and daunting process that is often rewarding and also frustrating and exhausting. But it did happen with Hope Meadows, and it can happen now. At the end of 2019, in over twenty states there were seven communities on the ground incorporating the basic tenets of intentional neighboring and twenty-five more in various stages of development. In looking ahead to more fully address the complex challenges faced by the change leaders of these communities and by our nation, we must begin to recognize two things:

- our nation's *social safety net*, based on the best efforts of business, government, and social services, still needs to be strengthened, and
- effective intervention into social problems requires a deep, holistic understanding of these problems acquired through *personal experiences and insights* of the people who live in our communities and neighborhoods.

To address both of these concerns, everyday people, regardless of age or vulnerability, must be an integral part of the solution.

Intentional neighboring is a powerful response to that need.

HOW SAFE IS AMERICA'S SOCIAL SAFETY NET?

We look to both public and private sectors to help those most vulnerable, to provide America's safety net. This assistance typically falls into four areas of need: food, income, housing, and health care; but these categories are proving to be inadequate. Dr. Mark Rank, a professor of social welfare at Washington University, writes that the US has "the weakest safety net among the Western industrialized nations, devoting far fewer resources as a percentage of gross domestic product to welfare programs than do other wealthy countries."[5]

As public and private sectors work to create and sustain a strong, healthy America, they continue to struggle to significantly reduce rates of poverty, especially among children, or to change the lives of so many older adults who daily face the deterioration of their health and happiness due to, as Dr. Bill Thomas writes, loneliness, boredom, and a pervasive sense of helplessness.[6] Nor do the policies and practices of our traditional safety net effectively address the problems related to homelessness, drug addiction, the cradle to prison pipeline, and most institutional care. Sufficient funding with proper oversight is certainly part of the solution, but there will never be money enough to eradicate our most serious social problems—problems that have become increasingly intractable and which beg for human solutions—for a new category of need.

Relationships: Fundamental to Wellbeing

I believe our safety net lacks a critical focus, a missing piece. If we are to have any hope for significant change in the lives of our most vulnerable citizens, a fifth category of need must be added—*the universal need for caring relationships*. Rarely do we think about the value and essential importance of caring relationships to our wellbeing, relationships like Al and Kenny had. Yet there is a substantial body of research showing that caring relationships are essential to *everyone's* emotional and physical health and to our happiness, and even, we are finding, to our longevity.

Vivek Murthy, the nineteenth Surgeon General of the United States, wrote in the *Harvard Business Review* that "Loneliness and weak social connections are associated with reduction in lifespan similar to that caused by smoking fifteen cigarettes a day and even greater than that associated with obesity."[7] Loneliness is so disabling that pursuing relationships is, as University of Pennsylvania psychologist, Marvin Seligman writes (referencing the late neuroscientist John Cacioppo), "a rock bottom fundamental to wellbeing."[8] And the highly insightful scholar, Kenneth J. Gergen argues that our own, community, and even global wellbeing depends on placing relationships at the forefront of the struggles of our time.[9]

Integrating Safety Net Sectors

Hope Meadows put relationships at its core, exploring a new organizational structure established to address what many deemed a national crisis: the crack epidemic. This new structure blurred many sectorial boundaries. It was a neighborhood established under the umbrella of a *nonprofit organization*. The nonprofit was, in part, a *business* utilizing rental income to help support its work, and it was a *child welfare agency* operating under *government* rules and regulations.

Recently I came across a paper titled *The Emerging Fourth Sector,* authored in 1996 by Heerad Sabeti with the Fourth Sector Network Working Group and supported by the Aspen Institute and the W.K. Kellogg Foundation. This new sector where business, government, and nonprofits converge was needed, Sabeti argued, because the three established sectors, each with their own "specialized support system," were not designed to meet many of the complex challenges (as well as opportunities) that we as a country faced. As such, our existing social safety net could not provide a foundation to support the growing number of multifaceted new organizations (including Generations of Hope), created to address these challenges—organizations requiring the *integration of all sectors* in order to carry out their missions.

Expectations that these new entities should be able to operate within traditional sectorial boundaries inevitably resulted in much frustration and disappointment. This is understandable, as fourth-sector organizations are designed, Sabeti imagined, to do the opposite: "to challenge conventional thinking" in the development of "new instruments, new institutions, and not least of all new understandings." These efforts would result in the fourth sector becoming, he concluded, "a beacon of possibility in a world in need of hope."[10]

I was relieved to come across Sabeti's work and found comfort in learning that in our early years we were actually in sync with some emerging cutting-edge ideas; Hope was not the only organization to join together key sectors of our safety net, square pegs trying to fit into one round hole. But from my vantage point twenty-five years later, it seems that most of these fourth sector organizations and institutions still rely primarily on politicians; professionals in medicine, education, and social services; philanthropic and business communities; lawyers and consultants—an army of professionals to define the problems we all face, design programs and implement solutions.

Adding A Fifth Sector

While Hope did indeed resemble a fourth sector hybrid, our operational paradigm (intentional neighboring) and the informal but essential workforce of neighbors it depended upon represent another key component—a new discipline of knowledge and practices—one that goes beyond the definition of Sabeti's model. To understand this is to appreciate that *the people next door can be as powerful as professionals in addressing serious social problems.*

Sabeti's fourth sector emphasizes the merged interests of business, government and social services, creating a hybrid and collaborative service model. But beyond the merging of professional sectors, Hope Meadows also employed the broader, inclusive capacities of nonprofessionals—the ordinary people living within it. We added the invaluable participation of neighbors who were not simply advisors, volunteers, or residents participating in a program, but who were fully involved and invested in the health and wellness of everyone in our Hope community.

The residents of Hope, with a *shared purpose, shared values, and relational leadership* became experts in addressing the underlying human suffering caused by isolation and loneliness and the role that close, dependable and daily relationships play in resilience and flourishing. Our professional staff listened to them, learned from them, and supported them, recognizing their important role in the work of Hope Meadows. Had we not viewed them as essential partners in the organization, its mission would have surely failed. Through their power, understandings, experiences, and knowledge of each other and with their innate capacity to care, the people of Hope Meadows possessed their own unique set of skills derived from meaningful relationships.

To strengthen our country's social safety net, this expertise, with its focus on relationships, must be woven into every system of professional support and service, becoming, it could be argued, the heartbeat of everyone's work. Built on broader and more inclusive human resources and capacities, our traditional safety net of services can be reconfigured to incorporate *a fifth sector, the skilled and sensitive workforce within our social institutions of family, neighborhoods, and communities.* Global nonprofit Ashoka refers to this workforce as the "citizen sector," which they define as "groups of citizens who care and act to serve others and [thereby] cause needed change."[11]

QUALIFICATIONS FOR THE JOB—EXPERIENCES AND INSIGHTS

Over time, through a dominant focus on neighboring, the people of Hope—including the children—came to be profoundly insightful and perceptive regarding one another's needs. The following four conversations with residents are included here, just in case the notion of neighbors as experts in human care seems far-fetched. Their simple words—so simple they can easily be overlooked and undervalued—express tremendous compassion and understanding for one another's needs and reflect the deep insights they had into the human heart.

Marcus, a boy without any sense of joy or adventure when he first arrived, explained why he loved living at Hope just two years later.

> Because it is fun. You can do things and go places. You can play at the park. I like to skate and ride my bike and scooter. It is fun at the basketball court. We went to see the Harlem Globetrotters. I like to ice skate at the rink. We took a trip to New York City. We took pictures of the

Statue of Liberty and we climbed to the top. We went to the University of Illinois and saw the stars and how big the moon was. We watched the whole roof move with the telescope! We went on a train to Champaign, had a picnic in the park, rode a city bus, caught a big bus and rode back to Rantoul. That's why I like living here.[12]

Miss Irene told us about how she and five-year-old Darcel shared deeply one afternoon.

Darcel asked me, 'You live alone, don't you?'

And I said, 'Yes, I do.'

He asked, 'Where is he?'

I said, 'Honey, he died.'

He then asked, 'Did you kill him?'

'No.'

'Did he get real sick?'

'Yes, he did.'

'Do you miss him?'

'Yes,' I said.

'Do you cry?'

'Yes.'

Then he said, 'I'll be your man.' And he went home and called me on the phone,

'I'm coming over, and I'm bringing my suitcase. You don't have a man in the house, and you need one.'[13]

Bill Biederman and little Grace played a daily game of trust and love.

Usually when she comes over to the house, I say, 'I love you Grace.'

> And she'll say, 'I love you too, Grandpa.'
>
> And I'll say, 'I love you more.'
>
> She'll say, 'No, I love you more.' And this goes on and on.[14]

Miss Irene shared Leon's favorite memories—ones he will treasure all of his life.

> I was tutoring Leon when out-of-the-blue he asked me, 'Grandma, do you remember when I was a little bitty boy and I looked at you and asked you, "Grandma, am I just wasting your time?" Look what I'm doing now! And remember, Grandma, when I lived in Sandy's house over there, and I helped you down the stairs because your hip was real sore?'
>
> 'Yes,' I said, 'I remember.'
>
> 'You got down to the bottom of the steps and you said, "Thank you, little man." And I looked at your face and you had tears in your eyes, Grandma.'[15]

Trusting relationships bloomed through *daily* acts of care and kindness, including "doing things and going places" with people of all ages from the neighborhood, listening, playing simple word games, and sharing memories. As the depth and intimacy of their interactions plainly show, our Hope children developed uncommon compassion and empathy. As seniors and parents shared stories and insights with each other and with staff, we all learned the lessons essential to an all-encompassing understanding of these children. Parents and grandparents knew what the children needed in their day-to-day lives and how to address these needs in ways no one else could. Imagine how much easier it would be for physicians, social workers, and therapists to do their work if they came equipped with the knowledge ordinary people can glean through being there for and with each other—through intentional neighboring.

WHAT'S IN OUR WAY?

If the people next door—namely all of us—are any kind of solution to the problems we face today, why on earth aren't we all enlisted to the cause? One reason is disbelief, caused in turn by lack of experience. While we understand family and the trendier notion of "my people," how many of us have developed close relationships with our neighbors, or built enduring friendships with people much older or younger than we are? Most of us assume that meaningful, caring relationships are best formed with members of one's nuclear or extended family, and then with people who have shared interests, histories, social status, age, race, or religion. We tend to gravitate to people like ourselves, so how can neighbors who don't fit this description be persons with whom we deeply share our lives?

60 Minutes correspondent Lesley Stahl had these very same doubts when she first visited Hope Meadows. When we spoke about her memoir, *On Becoming Grandma*, Lesley admitted that she had to see it to believe it: that people who were not related and so very different from one another could form such close and enduring "grandparenting" friendships.[16] These conventional beliefs about kinship and tribal relationships tend to foster narrow approaches to practices and policies as we fail to appreciate and therefore incorporate the profound benefits of caring relationships among neighbors.

Other reasons are imbedded in the very structures of our

systems of service. First, they are by necessity vast and sprawling to meet the needs of our vast and sprawling populations. More and more, they are governed by strong standards of care, and it goes to follow that professional services are the centerpiece of every system. To meet such high demand for care, virtually all social services are provider-driven and rely on outside professional expertise to be effective. Even with the move toward community-based services, most of these professionals have not been trained to work within an empowered community, to rely on the strengths of that community, and to support rather than direct community initiatives. Their education and prior work experience usually prepare them to take charge and make decisions in circumstances where their skills and knowledge apply and where it is assumed other participants (including parents) are not similarly equipped. The directionality of the intervention is clearly from the off-site professional to the individual or family.

In this environment and faced with high caseloads (often due to a shortage of qualified staff) and the complex needs of their patients and clients, professionals easily overlook the profound contributions everyday people of all ages and backgrounds can make to the wellbeing of one another. For example, while the outside professionals Hope worked with were certainly glad to see improvements in the health, behaviors and happiness of our children and our seniors, they rarely came to believe that the value of neighboring relationships at all compared to the worth of their own knowledge, training, expertise, and skill sets. As a result, these therapists, doctors, and social workers rarely tried to heal and help by utilizing the knowledge and experiences of the residents of the neighborhood. One or two pediatricians and a number of the children's teachers who often welcomed input from the "Grandpas" and "Grandmas" (with parent permission of course) were exceptions.

We all know how frustrating this approach can be.

Once, I tried to talk to a psychiatrist who was instrumental in admitting one of our Hope children to a local hospital. I wanted to tell him that Sammy had recently seen his birthmother at Walmart, and it had upset him terribly. I wanted to let him know that Sammy's dog had been sick—that the boy was afraid his dog would die—one more potential loss in a string of losses endured in his young life. I wanted to tell him about the Hope grandparents who had spent many hours with this child and had simply listened as he began to trust them, sharing his deepest fears and worries. They would come to the hospital to help if invited to do so. But the psychiatrist didn't listen; he probably didn't have time. *His system didn't work that way.* It was based on, as Gergen writes, "the presumption of knowledge as a condition of individual minds" rather than "*...knowledge as an outcome of relational processes.*"[17]

For too long we have ignored the value, importance and power of the people next door—especially of those who are vulnerable and those who are older—to help make this world a better place, not only for those facing difficult challenges, but for *all* of us. We have underestimated, underutilized, and too often completely ignored the importance of the special gifts, talents, experiences, and capacity to care that ordinary people through neighboring possess in helping to address adversities that make us vulnerable. We have forgotten that what gives our life its deepest significance and meaning are not professional services, but *the caring relationships* we make with family, friends, and neighbors. We have forgotten, as Christopher Alexander's writings continually remind us, of the "profound importance of the ordinary."[18]

In these troubled times, the stories from Hope Meadows and other intentional neighboring communities, along with our growing understanding of the importance of caring relationships to wellbeing, reinforce the value of intentional neighboring in healing and uniting us individually and as a fractured nation. As the evidence mounts, the call to the traditional keepers of our social safety net to change the way business is done as usual will only intensify.

To some, this vision of an expanded safety net and unity among its sectors may seem impossible. But like the Queen said to Alice, one can believe in impossible things. It is time to not only believe in the importance of neighboring where everyday people become as important as the professionals in the private and public sectors of our safety net, but also to *act* on this belief.

- Fourteen -

Intentional Neighboring: Looking Forward

> Neighborhood: A term that is hard to define precisely, but everyone knows it when they see it.[1]
>
> —Dr. George Galster, "On the Nature of Neighbourhood"

LETTING GO OF THE FAMILIAR

Large-scale change is required for diverse forms of intentional neighboring to become a "normal" part of America's landscape, a sought-after lifestyle option, and an integrated component of our social systems of care. This change is underway and in demand across this country and beyond. Whereas we once could only imagine a neighborhood where residents come alongside one another to address personal and social challenges through supportive relationships, the founding neighbors of Hope Meadows, Bastion, Bridge Meadows and others like it are showing us the way. Their stories not only validate the impact of intentional neighboring but over and over they show us how it can be achieved in daily life. They reflect core values and design patterns common to our human experience, with the power to resonate across every discipline.

Still, bridging the gap between proven models for change and current practices requires a new kind of thinking and acting on a broad scale. And how do we get there, when the work itself seems to ask us to think entirely differently about how we live together in homes, neighborhoods and in all kinds of communities, and even to redefine our notions of neighborhood altogether?

For many years, I thought almost solely about intentional neighboring within the context of what was *familiar* to me: a neighborhood of single-family homes clustered on a block or blocks or within a subdivision, consisting of people of various ages and family configurations, some raising children, some working, others retired—organically intergenerational. Within that context, Hope Meadows developed naturally to concentrate upon the needs of vulnerable children placed in foster/adoption families and surrounded by grandfriends.

But of course, vulnerability is not limited to children, nor are neighborhoods limited to clusters of single-family homes. When I finally let go of the constraints of familiarity, it didn't take long to imagine intentional neighboring as a response to all kinds of human problems as they emerge across the landscape of our culture, especially those problems that marginalize and isolate whole groups of people for their various differences. This response, based in purposeful connection, caring and support, is most naturally accomplished through proximal, daily relationships and thus perfectly suited for neighborhood life, regardless of setting. In truth, intentional neighboring can exist in any setting that includes homes and willing neighbors; as such, it can be an integral and foundational feature of almost any community-based system of support, from housing to healthcare. After all, what program designed to help any person or group—from young adults with autism to struggling immigrant families to persons with mental health challenges, or seniors with dementia—would not be enhanced if their "clients" lived in safe and affordable homes and belonged to a community of caring and supportive neighbors?

WE AND THE PEOPLE WE CARE ABOUT

My good friend's daughter Lisa, diagnosed with a serious mental illness at age eighteen, was one of those "clients." She died recently from complications resulting from her illness at the age of thirty-six. Time after time, our systems of care failed to meet Lisa's needs. She needed more than clinical and medical solutions; she needed a caring community of friends and neighbors.

Only in the last decade have we begun to understand the importance of community to people living with mental illness. A psychiatric researcher at the Yale School of Medicine, Dr. Larry Davidson was quoted in a February 2020 *New York Times* article on mental illness and recovery: "Personal recovery" (after receiving a mental-health diagnosis) "has as much to do with the quality of a person's sense of identity and belonging to community as it does to subjective experiences of mental illness."[2] Sadly, most people with chronic mental health challenges experience just the opposite—rather than identity rooted in belonging, the conditions of their experience more often lead to confusion, trauma, and isolation.

For individuals with autism and intellectual and developmental disabilities (I/DD), a similar experience of isolation exists, especially as they go through what many families describe as "falling off a cliff" upon graduation or aging out of public education. "From that moment," Deb Finck once told me, "any sense of belonging to a larger community beyond immediate family is ripped away, and more often than not, only painstakingly and partially rebuilt. This experience is as hurtful and traumatic as falling off a cliff."[3] Some of these adults go on to live independently, some in adult family homes or in other forms of supported living. But according to The ARC, a national policy and advocacy organization, an increasing number of adults with I/DD are living at home with their aging baby boomer parents, and without tremendous support they may not be able to avoid placement in costly and inappropriate institutions.[4] As this generation of parent-caregivers begin to age, they grow deeply concerned about the future of their children. A majority of the emerging intentional neighboring initiatives that I hear about are efforts to support these individuals (and their caregivers) through the creation of diverse and inclusive communities of support.

Beyond I/DD, the challenges for all aging caregivers in primary support roles is pervasive. One quickly growing demographic includes grandparents raising grandchildren. Nationwide, 2.6 million grandparents are currently raising grandchildren and about one-fifth of those have incomes that fall below the poverty line.[5] I am reminded of the young woman I met last year whose mother and father left her to be raised by her grandparents. This couple now face serious health issues and are no longer able to be primary caregivers, even as they continue to love their granddaughter, who recently became a mother herself. An intentional neighboring community, like Derenda Schubert's Bridge Meadows and New Meadows in Portland, Oregon, could embrace and support all three of these generations.

So too, could Genesis, a Generations of Hope inspired intentional neighboring community in Washington, DC. Launched in 2015, Genesis is home to young mothers who grew up in foster care and their children. These families live alongside seniors on fixed incomes and other community-minded families. The "neighborhood" is a 27-unit affordable rental apartment complex developed by Mi Casa in partnership with city agencies. Renovated to encourage intergenerational relationships, it features a community kitchen, meeting room, garden, and library. The job of the Genesis program staff is to facilitate engagement among all residents, provide individual support to all residents—the families, children, and seniors living there—and facilitate linkages to outside social services. Above all, it seems to be the neighboring that matters most. As one young mom reports on the Genesis website: "The relationships at Genesis help me see myself differently, to believe I can achieve my dreams and be there so my kids can too."[6]

SPECIALIZED "NEIGHBORHOODS OF CARE" FOR THE AGING

Any discussion that explores the benefits of intentional neighboring across a variety of social and health challenges must eventually lead to consideration of those very people who made Hope Meadows more than an isolated enclave of foster families: the seniors. Through their stories and actions, these residents show us both the power of relationships in aging well and why it is important to rethink the meaning of vulnerability—two core values of intentional neighboring. It is no mistake that seniors have been and will be integral to the stability, maturity and well-being of intentional neighborhoods of every shape and kind.

But what about the vast numbers of "senior neighborhoods" already in existence? Senior Care Communities come in all shapes and sizes; they include but are not limited to Continued Care Retirement Communities (CCRCs), group homes, assisted living and nursing home facilities. These senior care "neighborhoods" are designed as places to age alongside other older adults, and where various levels of care and assistance are provided in that journey. Many are built for long-term and end-of-life care, of which more and more specialize in dementia care (sometimes designated as Memory Care) like the one where my mother lived.

Within these senior care communities are diverse experiences of aging, and thus a need for many evolving levels of support. Elmer and Margie, for instance, were able to be active and independent at Hope, even with chronic health challenges, until they died. My mother, on the other hand, enjoyed vigorous physical health, but dementia drastically limited her freedom and thus her ability to live without 24-7 care.

In every circumstance and in all seasons of aging, I believe it is still possible to age well until the end of life. How we think about the worth and value of our aging citizens will be key to such an outcome, as our society's attitudes and beliefs always shape the trajectory of our social programs and policies. Sadly, many of our deeply-held beliefs and assumptions are rooted in "ageism," a term first coined by Robert Butler in 1969.[7] He wrote that like racism and sexism, ageism refers to stereotyping of and discrimination against people, in this case, just "because they are old." Many studies, including one published in 2015 in the *Journal of Geriatrics*, have found that "negative stereotypes" have deleterious effects on the physical and mental health of older people as well as to their sense of identity and belonging.[8] And yet, many of these negative stereotypes of weakness and helplessness power our service models of care for the aging, and for many of the groups discussed above.

Nowhere is this more evident than in the relationships between persons who need care and their care providers. Once older people need help, we automatically shift our relationship to them:

whatever it was before becomes a relationship between the "carer" and the "cared-for." This alteration can be seen in families most clearly, for example, when an aging parent who has enjoyed rich and mutually rewarding relationships is reduced to the beloved but helpless patient who can no longer be trusted to make their own decisions or contribute to the life of the household in meaningful way. But in order for senior care communities to be places where *all* people flourish—not just residents or patients, but all staff, family members, friends and community volunteers—the reciprocal practice of "social caring" must be added to traditional practices of care.

Acts of "social caring," be they in our own homes or in care communities, involve the emotional experience of concern on the part of the *carer* and a reciprocal emotional experience of gratitude on the part of the "*cared-for*." (This will occur even in circumstances where verbal communication is not possible.) As time passes, such a caring relationship will result in mutuality or reciprocity, as the carer and the cared-for exchange places as opportunities arise. To my mind, this is the relational dynamic at the heart of intentional neighboring. Barbara Tarlow, an eminent scholar on the theory of caring, writes:

> To be caring of one another provides witness to the sense of community, and of one's identity as part of it. Caring demonstrated, is yet one more instance of an acknowledgement of the respect for the meaning of the group. Caring can and does spread throughout the community, perhaps stopping here, but passing onto another there.[9]

Over time, as happened at Hope Meadows, long-held beliefs are replaced with the knowledge that everyone matters, everyone cares, and everyone belongs. These beliefs about ourselves and one another can change the way we view social services. David Racine says this well: "Hope Meadows has elements of a social program to be sure, but its essence is much more fundamental. In social programs you focus on the benefits to the people whom the program has been designed to help. Through intentional neighboring, everyone is supposed to benefit and in a significant way. That's why it works. That's why people are drawn to the idea."[10]

A FORMIDABLE CHALLENGE

All models for senior living are facing formidable challenges, including ever-increasing costs and regulations, the demands for high quality physical health and safety care, significant workforce shortages, and the complex needs of the growing numbers of people who are living longer and with Alzheimer's disease and other causes of dementia. These challenges are not dissimilar to those faced by DCFS in the 1980's (and again in 2020), as they tried to serve so many displaced children and youth. Against this backdrop, some argue that addressing psychosocial determinants of health (via such practices as social caring, for example) only exacerbates these challenges. I can only tell you that this was not the case at Hope Meadows, nor is it true for Hope & a Future in Wisconsin. In both of these communities, addressing the psychosocial needs of all of our residents appears to have resulted in greater health, greater happiness, and longer, more productive lives. Nonetheless, despite these benefits, more data is needed before the argument "in favor of" is finally won; for that to happen, we need more demonstrations of intentional neighboring in all its forms.

ONCE AGAIN, NO SMALL THING

In order to gain participation and partnership within social services and other safety net sectors, we need more communities of intentional neighboring on the ground. This is no small endeavor, as the cost of development in both private and publicly funded markets is complex and expensive. The impetus for creating these communities often arises from grassroots or community-based awareness of need. Across the country families are looking for housing and support options for their adult children with autism, for instance; or a community nonprofit or agency sees the need for inclusive community to support a marginalized constituency, as happened with Genesis.

It's not uncommon for these projects to take years to get off the ground. This is because securing the land, the partnerships, and the development financing for an entirely new housing market requires community buy-in and cooperation from regulatory bodies, municipalities, cities, and state governments. The lion's share of specialized and supportive housing is built with public monies and by affordable housing developers; and, publicly funded affordable housing comes with its own body of required expertise and is really its own industry. It is only in the last few years that restrictive zoning and development regulations are relaxing to allow for more freedom in community design and more flexibility in allowing appropriate density, more mixed-use developments, cottage and right-sized home styles, and blended neighborhood housing for more economically diverse housing projects.

Finding land with the right criteria can be challenging but not impossible. Intentional community developments can be built on or near college campuses, in small towns adding to revitalization efforts, or in urban or suburban high-rises including those once occupied by a large company or corporation and now vacated. They can be built utilizing brown fields, land owned by religious institutions, abandoned schools, or closed malls and surrounding parking lots. More and more project leaders are looking for land that is accessible, closer to parks, community gathering centers, transportation, shopping and jobs, as an inclusive neighborhood also seeks to be connected and integral to the life of their wider community.

One new supportive housing project is underway in South Bend Indiana, where the city's Board of Public Works has gifted to non-profit, Village-to-Village International, five city-owned adjacent vacant lots to build duplexes for a project based on intentional neighboring. This is part of a revitalization effort that has been under way for several years. The executive director of a nonprofit neighborhood organization where this property is located is quoted as saying, "I think this [project] is going to flow right into the neighborhood and most people won't understand the mission of the place; they'll just know they're good neighbors."[11] As in South Bend, project advocates in New Orleans, and in many other states are working in concert with state Housing Authorities and real estate developers who specialize in the creation of sustainable, connected neighborhoods.

Opportunities to create newly constructed intentional neighborhoods also exist in the realm of private market development. According to recent industry surveys, over 1000 large scale, master planned mixed-use communities are underway and slated for development in 2020, creating neighborhoods for over 1.7 million homes.[12] On the west coast, some private market developers and designers of planned residential and mixed-use communities are exploring how they might incorporate intentional neighborhoods into their larger visions, recognizing their role in the creation of healthier, more inclusive communities for our future. They understand that inclusive communities must also be organically responsive to the needs of people, and that planned development can not only support but enhance the relationships so crucial to intentional neighboring, to individual and community wellbeing.

I had the opportunity to work with one such developer in 2017, Newland Communities. They joined hands with Building Ohana in Spokane, Washington as the hosts of a two-day charette to envision and create a site plan for a one-of-a-kind mixed-use development: including various micro- and pocket neighborhoods; walkable throughout with shared greenspaces and trails; built with neighborhood business development in mind; and, planned with Ohana Village at its heart, an intentional neighborhood where people with intellectual and developmental disabilities will thrive alongside their neighbors. This remarkable gathering was co-facilitated by two gifted Washington architects: Jonathan Davis, designer of the award-winning Grow Community on Bainbridge Island,[13] and Ross Chapin, the author of *Pocket Neighborhoods: Creating Small-Scale Community in a Large-Scale World*. Both of these professionals came to this project with a deep understanding of the power of the people next door. Ross writes that "Pocket neighborhoods can re-establish communities where nearby neighbors can respond to daily needs in a way that friends across town and family across the country cannot—mending webs of belonging, care, and support needed in a frayed world."[14]

As micro- and pocket neighborhoods had their beginnings in Europe, so did the cohousing movement—a model for cooperative housing and shared lifestyle brought from Denmark in the 1970's by architects Katie McCamant and Chuck Durrett.[15]

Historically a resident-led, private market development model, cohousing has over the past several years been challenged to build diversity and affordability into their cooperative neighborhoods. Although cohousing was not conceived specifically to support vulnerable populations, helping one another emerges organically through the cohousing lifestyle, and thus more and more like-minded cohousers are imagining ways to add more focused and planned levels of support for residents in both new and established communities. In this respect, cohousing and communities like Hope, Bastion and the future Ohana are becoming more closely aligned in their intentions. In Portland, Oregon one new cohousing townhouse project seeks to provide a portion of its housing to families and individuals living with developmental disabilities,[16] and near Charlottesville, Virginia a cohousing project is being designed to address needs of young adults with mental illnesses.[17]

EXISTING COMMUNITY MODELS

Communities with new construction and new financing methods are only part of what is needed. New challenges and opportunities also exist to push the envelope by exploring ways to realize the underlying goals of intentional neighboring in *already established* buildings and neighborhoods. Genesis took over an already existing multi-story building. New Life Village, located on 11.8 acres of land near Tampa, Florida consists of thirty-two already existing town-homes. As the program evolves, more homes will be built.[18]

Dr. Niranjan Karnik, at Rush University's Medical College in Chicago and a nationally recognized expert on community behavioral health, is exploring how intentional neighboring can be applied to long-established neighborhoods where people have lived side-by-side for years in urban dwellings. With substantial support from foundations and the University, Dr. Karnik's project is working to infuse intentional neighboring into a nearby underserved neighborhood. His professional team will be working with local residents who have emerged as leaders, guiding them as they use the tenants of this model, especially older adults, to support neighbors challenged by trauma, stress, poverty, and violence.

Intentional neighboring is in its infancy, but as the work of Dr. Karnik, innovative private and affordable housing developers like Mi Casa, and many others are showing, it is evolving and will continue to evolve and change over time, always guided by core values and key design patterns. No community will be the same. And it will be daunting work, because with every new iteration of intentional neighboring, whether it be infused into revitalization projects, senior care facilities or existing neighborhoods, or planted as the humanity-based centerpiece for care within new private and/or public housing developments, leaders will have to address the ingrained practices of mavens of housing, community development, aging, and social services. But there is hope.

REGENERATING THE HUMAN SPIRIT

On-the-ground successes will generate new conversations by safety net experts—including the people next door—to examine current approaches in every aspect of our safety net of services. Years of experience have taught us that two simple but important questions are needed to guide these conversations. First is the same personal question we asked when we were just forming Hope Meadows: "If this decision impacted my loved ones, would I still make the same decision?" The second relates to the formation of relationships within community. "Are public policies and practices contributing to the formation of supportive, inclusive, intergenerational relationships, especially within community and through this, as Dr. Thomas writes, "the regeneration of the human spirit?"[19]

These two questions are critical and should be asked at every juncture, keeping us on track and mindful of our purposes. Answers can hit home with unwavering precision: "No." is simply unacceptable. The asking and answering of these questions also create a radical shift of focus from professional interventions designed to remediate individual problems toward inclusive interventions tapping the power of the people next door—including those in need—to create nurturing environments for mutual wellbeing.

Only by all sectors gathering—not only in corporate offices, but in neighborhoods as well—to define problems, explore possible solutions, and foster collective wellbeing will the solving of social issues be democratized. Only then will we all be legitimately empowered to participate in finding and implementing solutions to some of our most difficult social problems. And only then will the general public no longer feel like bystanders wondering, "Why bother?", for it will be actually possible to believe in a future with real and abiding solutions that emerge from a true sense of harmony, equity, caring, integrity and hope.

Epilogue

So much has changed at Hope Meadows in the years since I left—board members, staff, and many of the residents. All are strangers to me with the exception of Kenny and Debbie Calhoun, the very first parents to move to Hope, and a handful of the founding seniors who are now in their eighties and early nineties. No longer a state-licensed child welfare agency, Hope has also changed its mission. It now supports highly fragile young families, some of whom have members with very serious medical conditions. Even the beautiful old trees which graced our streets are gone, having succumbed to Dutch Elm disease.

As time has passed and with so many changes both at Hope and in my life, I rarely visit there anymore. Every year, however, I do go to the Memorial Garden where I sit on one of the two benches my dear friend and assistant Carolyn Casteel and I placed there so many years ago. In the garden is an engraved brick for everyone who lived at Hope Meadows and who passed away. There are older bricks—for Larry, George, Bill, and so many others, and newer bricks for those who have more recently died. Soon one will be placed there for Miss Irene. As I sit I am often brought to tears of sadness at the passing of so many who were dear to me, and tears of joy at remembering the unexpected decency, kindness, and just plain goodness of these everyday people, who daily—in being their best selves—transformed the ordinary into the extraordinary.

From the Memorial Garden I walk two blocks to the far edge of the playground to the site where Elmer's and Margie's ashes lie. Close to the resting place of these dear people, I know that they and so many others would agree with the words of Miss Irene when she told me, "[Here] I feel useful; I feel I have a purpose. When my life is over on earth, I know I've left something of value behind."

I made this pilgrimage once again not long ago. It was a beautiful sunny afternoon, nothing like the wintry day when I first met Elmer. As I walked back to my car I was overwhelmed with gratitude for the memories the people of Hope Meadows had given me, for the lessons they had taught me and for the joy I felt in knowing I had helped to make a difference in their lives and they in mine.

During my forty-minute drive home, it occurred to me that I had entered into yet another transitional decade. "Certainly now," I thought, "my work is over. Eighteen months into retirement, Wayland and I love having time with our children and precious grandchildren, and we love the freedom that retirement brings to do what we want when we want. *But still...* "

Then I had yet one more *aha* moment.

I still needed a life of worth beyond family, friends, gardening, reading, and baking. My work wasn't over! I could continue to make a difference in the lives of others and be inspired by others as well. My daughter Sarah had just sent me a card inscribed with the well-known quote about believing in impossible things from *Through the Looking Glass*. Sarah wrote, "Thank you for always believing in 'impossible things' and for always encouraging me to do the same."

Thinking of Sarah's note and remembering the people of Hope Meadows, I knew that my new job was to encourage future change leaders to believe in their ability to make the impossible possible—to believe in themselves and in their visions for compassionate intergenerational communities, communities where a tapestry of relationships built over time and with care and commitment thrived, and where the promise and power of the people next door could be realized.

More than ever before, I thought, we need these leaders with their visions for systems change. Hope Meadows was a trailblazer, but it will take an entire new generation of leaders and communities before there is really meaningful change—before intentional neighboring finally becomes a way of life. Just as I pulled into the driveway, my cell phone rang. It was Deb with some encouraging news about Ohana, asking me for just a small piece of advice. Like Esther, I thought to myself, "I really do have a wonderful life."

Acknowledgements

The story of Hope Meadows and all of its wisdom is a collective one, built of the families who inspired it, the people who lived there, and those who worked tirelessly to make it a reality on the ground.

I am grateful to all of the parents and children who trusted me with their stories in the '80s, no matter how painful or disturbing. And I am especially grateful to the founding residents of Hope Meadows, whose caring, sacrifice, perseverance, kindness and joy remain a tribute to the human spirit and whose friendship will always remain with me as a treasured gift.

I am also grateful to all of the many board members with whom I have worked. Your sacrifices of time and energy and your dedication to Hope's mission is greatly appreciated. Special thanks go to the original board members of Hope for the Children: Dr. Rebecca Wagner, Reverend Charles Nash, Dr. Napolean Knight, and Judi and Rudi Laufhuette; and to board members Kirk Harney, Jim Noland, and David Thies for their commitment and perseverance once Hope Meadows was established.

At the heart of this book is the primary importance of caring relationships. I am truly blessed by the friendships of Hope collaborators, whose caring support has been a cherished gift. By my side throughout this long journey have been two very special colleagues—Drs. Martha Bauman Power and David Hopping. Your friendship, brilliant insights, and hard work have meant everything to me. I am also grateful to Drs. David Racine, Elissa Mitchell, Niranjan Karnik, and Georgette Page for your commitment to an evolving experiment and for your ongoing observations and research. All of you made the years we spent together extraordinarily gratifying; laughing; continually challenging each other to think creatively and outside the box; being there for each other in times of deadlines, joyous occasions, and personal sorrow; and performing daily acts of kindness (David H. bringing Marty and me a fresh cup of coffee every afternoon at two will never be forgotten). So too do I want to recognize and thank Carolyn Casteel. No one sacrificed more nor worked harder to make Hope Meadows a success than you. Much more than an assistant, for forty years you have been a treasured friend and confidant.

Without the help of Betsy Mitchell and the late John Hirschfeld, Hope Meadows might never have been more than a dream. Both worked tirelessly over many years to help Hope Meadows gain the support of the Illinois legislature, and both introduced me to some special people who became dear friends and strong supporters of Hope. John introduced me to Tracy Nugent, who has always been there whenever I needed great legal advice or just someone with whom I could talk to get me through a difficult situation. Betsy introduced me to Tom Berkshire, whose sense of humor, knowledge of DCFS, and efforts to promote the work of Generations of Hope never cease. I also want to express my appreciation to Mark Dunham, who introduced me to the halls of Congress and to many D.C. leaders. Your belief in the promise of intentional neighboring is unshakable.

It was journalist Wes Smith who first drew national attention to Hope Meadows through a front-page story in the *Chicago*

Tribune and then through his book, *Hope Meadows*. I can't thank you enough for your belief in our work and your seminal publications.

I owe enormous gratitude to Ted Chen, who tirelessly championed the expansion of our work to the W.K. Kellogg Foundation a source of generous support for many years. And I want to thank Dr. Bill Thomas, Marc Freedman, and Helene Block Fields, all leading experts in the field of aging well and strong advocates of our work. I am so grateful to all of you for your support and friendship.

I deeply appreciate the time given and the feedback I have received from readers of my manuscript: Jennifer Berkshire, Susan Karol Martel, Janet Stambolian, and colleagues already mentioned—David Hopping, Tom Berkshire, and Helene Block Fields. I especially want to thank Building Ohana founder Deborah Finck, who forced me with gentle nudges and brilliant insights to write and rewrite paragraphs, sections, and chapters of the manuscript. Deb is my editor extraordinaire whose advice, guidance, and never-ceasing encouragement have been invaluable. An added bonus has been our deepening camaraderie professionally and personally.

Finally, to my husband Wayland, and to our children Sarah and Seth, thank you is inadequate. Wayland has been by my side, always supporting me throughout my initial research, my years with Generations of Hope, and with the writing of this book. You have listened to me, encouraged me, and offered sage advice and opinions including on this manuscript. Your steadfast belief in me, Sarah's numerous phone calls each week over the years just to stay in touch and to tell me "I love you," and Seth's patience and laughter with me when I have called him over and over again for computer help has brought me a profound sense of wellbeing—of love, support, and belonging.

Like so much that I have written about in this book, it would not have been possible without the cherished friendships I have made and the love of my family.

Endnotes

Opening Quote

1 **"Human relations are"** ... Fred Rogers, *The World According to Mister Rogers: Important Things to Remember* (New York: Hachette Books, 2014), 94.

Introduction

1 **"Hope is not the same"** ... Václav Havel & Karel Hvizdala, *Disturbing the Peace: A Conversation with Karel Hvizdala* (New York: Knoff, 1986), 110.

2 **"I've had open-heart surgery"** ... Interview with Elmer, "Hope for the Children," *Nightline*, aired October 3, 1996, American Broadcasting Company.

3 ***grandfriends* like Elmer and Margie** ... The term grandfriend was coined by Helene Block Fields in her book, *Don't Cheat the Children: Connecting Generations Through GrandFriendships* (Downers Grove, Illinois: Wonderstone Press, 2009).

4 **But management and software design** ... Tom DeMarco and Timothy Lister, *Peopleware: Productive Projects and Teams* (New York: Dorset House Publishing, 1987),4. This foundational book is in its third edition, the latest printed in 2013.

5 **"Western heritage, particularly"** ... Ibid., 156.

6 **"...so old-fashioned, it's"** ... Ted Koppel, "Hope for the Children," *Nightline*, aired October 3, 1996, American Broadcasting Company.

7 **"We read the news"** ... Courtney Martin, "Don't Look Away," *The Onbeing Project* (blog), September 14, 2017, **https://www.onbeing.org/blog/courtney-martin-dont-look-away/.**

Part I: Now and Then, Over and Over Again

1 **"An enhanced social science"** ... US Representative George Brown Jr., Chairman of the House Committee on Science, Space and Technology, "Quotable," *The Chronicle of Higher Education* (June 14, 1994), B5.

Chapter One

1 **"A Catalogue of Horrors"** … Jim Dey, "New DCFS Report Contains a Catalogue of Horrors," *The News-Gazette*, January 9, 2020, A1.

2 **"*We, Illinois, must do better.*"** … Meryl Paniak, acting inspector general at the Department of Children and Family Services, *Report to the Governor and the General Assembly of Illinois*, January 2020, executive letter.

3 **"so-called personal failures"** … Nicholas Kristof and Sheryl WuDunn, *Tightrope: Americans Reaching for Hope* (New York: Alfred A Knopf, Penguin Random House LLC, 2020), 66.

4 **"undercurrent of self-hatred,"** … Sarah Smarsh, "Chronicling a Community, and a Country, in Economic Crisis," *The New York Times*, January 10, 2020, BR1.

5 **"once you lose your"** … Atul Gawande, *Being Mortal: Medicine and What Matters in the End (*New York: Metropolitan Books, 2014), 75.

6 **"awake each morning and know"** … Dr. William Thomas, *What Are Old People For? How Elders will Save the World* (Acton, MA: VanderWyk & Burnham, 2004), 83.

7 **"I keep hoping that"** … Comments during DCFS parent training class, January 1983. This and all following citations through this and the next chapter named as "Interview" are taken from transcribed research interviews conducted over several years.

8 **"I wasn't warming up"** … Interview with foster parents, January 26, 1984.

9 **"The most disquieting thing"** … Ibid.

10 **"I just assumed that"** … Interview with foster parents, November 29, 1984.

11 **"I think DCFS discouraged"** … Interview with foster parents, January 26, 1984.

12 **"If you say no to"** … Ibid

13 **"We leave it a lot"** … Interview with DCFS social worker, May 4, 1984.

Chapter Two

1 **"Love is not only"** … Andrew Solomon, *Far from the Tree* (New York: Scribner, 2012), 582.

2 **"The biggest thing is"** … Interview with Dave and Sue Sheppard, foster/adopt parents, January 26, 1984.

3 **"Frustration marks every attempt"** … Interview with Dave and Sue Sheppard, foster/adopt parents, October 1984.

4 **"We do not love"** ... Interview with Dave and Sue Sheppard, foster/adopt parents, April 16, 1984.

5 **"We'd had a day where"** ... Interview with Sue Sheppard, February 17, 1985.

6 **"I love you. "** ... Letter given to author and Marty Power, February 17, 1985.

7 **"We realized that we"** ... Letter given to author and Marty Power, February 17, 1985.

8 **"When John came to live"** ... Interview with Sheppard parent, 1988.

9 **"He was like his"** ... Interview with Pat Johnson, foster mom, June 23, 1983.

10 **"It doesn't make any"** ... Ibid.

11 **"how to scold me"** ... Interview with Sam, April 21, 1984.

12 **"called the operator"** ... Ibid.

13 **"Sam came out and he"** ... Interview with Pat Johnson, foster mom, August 2, 1984.

14 **"I'm in this thing"** ... Interview with Dick Johnson, August 2, 1984.

15 **"Sam is such an outgoing"** ... Extended interview with Pat and Dick Johnson, February 26, 1985.

16 **"We can't do the same"** ... Bill and Melinda Gates Foundation website, **https://www.gatesfoundation.org**.

17 **"living through a social crisis"** ... Yuval Levin, "How Did Americans Lose Faith in Everything?" *The New York Times,* January 19, 2020, SR4.

Chapter Three

1 **"What the best and"** ... John Dewey, *The School and Society* (Chicago: University of Chicago Press, 1900), 19.

2 **"We don't get to know"** ... Interview with DCFS social worker, May 4, 1984.

3 **"I didn't study the family"** ... Interview with DCFS social worker, December 4, 1984.

4 **"When Brenda first sat down"** ... Wes Smith, *Hope Meadows: Real-life Stories of Healing and Caring from an Inspiring Community* (New York: The Berkley Publishing Group, 2001), 29-30.

5 **"When you reach the end"** ... variously attributed to Franklin Delano Roosevelt, Thomas Jefferson and others.

Chapter Four

1 **"Our children's very future"** ... Helene Block Fields, *Don't Cheat the Children: Connecting Generations Through GrandFriendships* (Downers Grove, Illinois: Wonderstone Press, 2009), 7.

2 **Following are the stories** ... Background information on Marcus and Kenny was taken from DCFS files given to Hope for the Children at the time of their referrals, 1995-1996.

3 **"Every day Marcus would come"** ... Eileen quoted in Rob Gurwitt, *Raising a Neighborhood* (San Francisco: Civic Ventures Innovations, 2001), 14.

4 **Yesterday, Sue Brown came** ... Notes from report by Hope for the Children's Afterschool Coordinator, 2001.

5 **"DCFS is no longer"** ... Kenny's written response to our question, "What does adoption mean to you?" November 27, 2000.

6 **"It was a challenge"** ... MaryAnn Daly in report to author about her work with children at Hope Meadows, April 2005.

7 **"Relationships," the late** ... widely acknowledged words of Peter Benson, former president and CEO of the Search Institute. I found it on a bookmark listing eight categories of "great things all kids need."

Chapter Five

1 **"When I read or hear"** ... Donna Holmes quoted in Barth, R. & M. Berry, *Adoption and Disruption: Rates, Risks, and Responses* (New York: Aldine DeGruyter, 1988), 183.

2 **"There," she confessed** ... Elsa Raab quoted in Wes Smith, *Hope Meadows: Real-life Stories of Healing and Caring from an Inspiring Community* (New York: The Berkley Publishing Group, 2001), 158.

3 ***The Adoption Symphony*** ... Poem given to author by Elsa Raab, Summer 2003.

4 **"high levels of motivation"** ... Urie Bronfenbrenner, "Who Cares for Children?" UNESCO, (Paris, September 7, 1989), 30.

5 **"Having kids—is the biggest"** ... Maria Shriver, "Quotable Quotes," *Goodreads,* **https://www.goodreads.com/quotes/276010-having-kids-the-responsibility-of-rearing-good-kind-ethical.**

6 **"Dear Brenda, These are"** ... Hand written note in pencil to author, March 12, 1997.

7 **"One night, after the children"**... Bev's story is pieced together from interviews with neighbors in the days following her husband's death (May 1997), and a later conversation between the author and Bev (November 1997)

8 ***adverse childhood experience*** ... A study by Kaiser Permanente in San Diego and the Centers for Disease Control over the lifespan of more than 17,000 individuals led to our understanding of adverse childhood experiences (ACE) including abuse and neglect, growing up with domestic violence, parental

addiction or mental illness, incarceration of a family member and divorce. For more information on this topic, read Nadine Burke Harris, M.D., *The Deepest Well: Healing the Long-Term Effects of Childhood Adversity* (Houghton Mifflin Harcourt, Boston, 2018).

9 **"How can I believe"** ... Letter sent to author from Dwayne, August 18, 2010.

Chapter Six

1 **"Lacking a coherent view"** ... Atul Gawande, *Being Mortal: Medicine and What Matters in the End* (New York: Metropolitan Books, 2014), 9.

2 "**If the parents were the true heroes** ... The stories that follow were pieced together from the following sources: the King story from transcripts of conversations with George King (September 5,1991) and his wife Effie (September, 1998); Esther's story from interviews with Esther, conducted by the author and Marty Power, March 17, 2005; combined with material from Wes Smith's book, *Hope Meadows: Real-life Stories of Healing and Caring from an Inspiring Community* (New York: The Berkley Publishing Group, 2001), 171-180; and letters in Hope's newsletter, *Seedlings*, March 18, 2002. Steve's story is taken from a letter written for the *Hope Herald* (Hope's national newsletter), Winter Issue, 2003; and from conversations with Steve's wife with author, September 9, 2017.

3 **Within two years, all** ... Data from *Hope for the Children Progress Report*, July - December, 2006.

4 **Approximately half of the seniors** ... Data from *Hope for the Children Progress Report*, January - June 1997.

5 **"We serve, we are"** ... Sherwin Nuland, *The Art of Aging: A Doctor's Prescription for Well-Being* (New York: Random House, 2007), 176.

6 **Marc Freedman, a proven** ... Talmud quote and Mark's observations in a letter to author through Encore.org., September 30, 2018.

7 **"Who they were"** ... David Racine made this comment to colleagues many times when speaking of Hope Meadows' seniors, 1997-2000.

Chapter Seven

1 **"Government can create"** ... David Brooks, "What Moderates Believe," *The New York Times*, August 22, 2017, A21.

2 **"We spend time together daily"** ... From a letter written to author, November 18, 2005.

3 **One such person was Janice** ... Informal conversation and interview with author, October 8, 2003.

4 **Many spoke of their** … Ben's poem was read at Janice's memorial service, October 22, 2007.

5 **"Good Morning, My wife"** … Transcribed testimony by Hope resident Jim Saunders before Illinois Appropriations Human Services Committee, March 20, 1998.

Chapter Eight

1 **"Many different kinds"** … *"The History of Vulnerability in the United States,"* Institute for Alternative Futures, May 4, 2018, 28-29. Download available at **https://nanopdf.com/download/the-history-of-vulnerability-in-the-united-states_pdf**.

2 **"For a long time"** … Ellen interviewed on *60 Minutes II, aired on* April 17, 2002, Columbia Broadcasting System.

3 **Over time, the vast** … Timothy Shriver, *Fully Alive: Discovering What Matters Most* (New York: Sarah Crichton Books, 2014), 268.

4 **"No community can flourish"** … Susan McFadden and John McFadden, *Aging Together* (Baltimore: Johns Hopkins University Press, 2011), 184.

Chapter Nine

1 **"Engagement…enhances the"** … Shelia Zedlewski and Simone G. Schaner, "The Retirement Project: Perspectives on Productive Aging," *Urban Institute,* May 6, 2006. Download available at: **https://www.urban.org/research/publication/older-adults-engaged-volunteers**.

2 **"The real secret of"** … George E. Valliant, M.D. (quoting Edmund Sanford), *Aging Well* (Boston: Little Brown and Company, 2002), 324.

3 **"Nothing much is expected"** … Email correspondence from David Racine to author, Fall 2016.

4 **"The children have done"** … Beverly Levitt (quoting Elmer), "Generations of Healing: Program Matches Older Residents with Foster Kids," *The States, AARP Regional News,* December 2000, 10.

5 **"When we know we"** … Wendy Lustbader, *Life Gets Better: The Unexpected Pleasures of Growing Old* (New York: Jeremy P. Tarcher/Penguin, 2011), 67.

6 **One year later, just** … Conversation between Elmer and author, close to his death, July 12, 2004.

7 **"Grandpa Elmer was very"** … Transcription of Kate's talk at Elmer's memorial service, August 6, 2004.

8 **"Joe worked hard as"** … "Memories of Joe Stang," *Seedlings,* December 2014.

9 **"At the Hope playground"** ... Rob Gurwitt, "Fostering Hope," *Mother Jones*, March/April Issue, 2002. Archived online at **https://www.motherjones.com/politics/2002/03/fostering-hope/**.

10 **"Generosity calls us to"** ... Wendy Lustbader, *Life Gets Better: The Unexpected Pleasures of Growing Old* (New York: Jeremy P. Tarcher/Penguin, 2011), 66.

11 **"At the beginning of the day"** ... David Racine, with Brenda Krause Eheart, David Hopping, Martha Bauman Power & Elissa Thomann Mitchell, "Generations of Hope Communities," *Generations of Hope White Paper Series*, Vol. II No. 2, 2008.

12 **The following senior engagement** ... Every six months an in-house progress report was compiled. As part of this document, senior engagement data and policies were summarized. To gather this information, we utilized "Formal Contact with Children" forms filled out by seniors; monthly "Volunteer Activity Logs;" and "Monthly Data Sheets for Seniors" which included participation in special events for the month and a summary of volunteer tasks and hours performed.

13 **"You are never alone"** ... Irene Bohn, quoted in an interview with the American Mural Project, June 2005.

Chapter Ten

1 **"I've found immense solace"** ... Visiting journalist, in a letter to Hope, printed in Hope's semiannual national newsletter, *Hope Herald*, Fall/Winter 2001.

2 **"'These youngsters come in'"** ... Lizbeth Schorr quoting Father James Harvey in *Within Our Reach: Breaking the Cycle of Disadvantage* (New York: Doubleday, 1989), 140.

3 **"The table was set"** ... From a thank-you letter written by a resident of Hope and printed in *Seedlings*, December 29, 2008.

4 **"Here are just two"** ... Author and Marty Power received copies of these letters from Fran Biederman, January 2004.

5 **"Grandma Esther was my"** ... Written by a Hope child, June 20, 2009.

6 **"I said goodbye to"** ... Poem written by Al Pena, August 1, 2003.

7 **"Just for you."**... Interview with author and Marty Power, February 4, 2002.

Chapter Eleven

1 **"Vision is the basic"** ... Beth Jarman and George Land, "Beyond Breakpoint: Possibilities for New Community," *Community Building: Renewing Spirit & Learning in Business* (San Francisco: Sterling & Stone, Inc., 1995), 32.

2 **"When they first found"** ... Interview with author and Marty Power, August 27, 2003.

3 **"I love the fact"** ... Interview with author and Marty Power, October 22, 2003.

4 **This diagram and those** ... Brenda Krause Eheart, David Hopping, Niranjan Karnik, Elissa Thomann Mitchell & Martha Bauman Power. Figures 1, 2, and 3 were created by David Hopping and first appeared in "Generations of Hope Communities: Augmenting Social Services with Neighborhood Care," *Generations of Hope White Paper Series*, Vol. II, No. 3, 2012, 11.

5 **"is primary and it"** ... David Racine in an email exchange with David Hopping and author, September 8, 2016.

6 **"There's joy in a life"** ... David Brooks, *The Road to Character* (New York: Random House, 2015), 269.

7 **"As proximity and commitment"** ... retrieved from W.K. Kellogg Foundation website, 2008, **https://www.wkkf.org**.

8 **"As I read, I wept"** ... A film producer, in a letter to Hope, printed in the semiannual national newsletter, *Hope Herald*, Fall/Winter 2001.

9 **change leaders** ... a term coined by Bill Drayton, founder of Ashoka, a global nonprofit that identifies and invests in leading social entrepreneurs.

10 **One of the first** ... Bridge Meadows in Portland, Oregon. See their website for more information: **https://www.bridgemeadows.org**.

11 **"The trauma of war"** ... conversation with Dylan Tête, founder and executive director of Bastion: A Community of Resilience in New Orleans, Louisiana. See the Bastion website: **https://www.joinbastion.org**.

12 **Karin Krause** ... Karin is the founder and director of Hope & a Future in Madison, Wisconsin. This story and more information about her community can be found at **https://www.hopeandafutureinc.org**.

13 "**In theory, community-based"** ... Deb Finck, founder and director of Building Ohana in Spokane, Washington. See Building Ohana website, **https://www.buildingohana.org**, January, 2018.

14 **Building Ohana publishes this list** ... "The Challenges We Face," retrieved from the Building Ohana website, **https://www.buildingohana.org/path-to-inclusion**, January, 2018.

Chapter Twelve

1 **"Caring can be learned"** ... Mary Catherine Bateson, *Composing a Life* (New York: Grove Press, 1989), 161.

2 **Design patterns are** … Christopher Alexander, Murray Silverstein, Shlomo Angel, Sara Ishikawa, Danny Abrams, *The Oregon Experiment* (New York: Oxford University Press, 1979), 16 -18.

3 **"Together they form"** … David Hopping writing for the Generations of Hope website, **https://ghdc.generationsofhope.org/components**, 2018.

4 ***"to change what would happen"*** … Christopher Alexander, *The Timeless Way of Building*, (New York: Oxford University Press, 1979), 14.

5 **"I think the reason people"** … Interview with the author and Marty Power, June 7, 1997.

6 **"It is like we are all"** … W.K. Kellogg Foundation video, *Profile of Hope Meadows*, 2007. View at **https://youtu.be/6eu86KbSMww**.

7 **Christopher Alexander's work** … Christopher Alexander, *The Timeless Way of Building* (New York: Oxford University Press, 1979).

8 **In his recently published** … Eric Klinenberg, *Palaces for the People: How Social Infrastructure Can Help Fight Inequality, Polarization, and the Decline of Civic Life* (New York: Crown, 2018), 5.

9 **"circle of care"** … For more on the "circle of care" concept see Brenda Krause Eheart, David Hopping, Martha Bauman Power & Colleen Vojak, "Completing the Circle of Care: Alternative Housing at Hope Meadows," *Generations of Hope Development Corporation White Paper Series*, Vol. 1, No. 2, June 2007, revised March 2010.

10 **"Both my boys"** … Interview with the author, August 10, 2003.

11 **This is in part because** … Eric Klinenberg, *Palaces for the People: How Social Infrastructure Can Help Fight Inequality, Polarization, and the Decline of Civic Life* (New York: Crown, 2018), 14.

12 **social infrastructure "becomes most visible"** … Ibid., 14.

13 **"I learned that Leon"** … This story was first told in an interview with David Hopping and Judith Pintar, November 14, 1997. It was to be repeated over and over through the years.

14 **in 2007, American sociologist** … Michael Jonas, writing about research by Robert Putnam, in "The Downside of Diversity: A Harvard political scientist finds that diversity hurts civic life. What happens when a liberal scholar unearths an inconvenient truth?" *The Boston Globe*, August 5, 2007. **http://www.boston.com/news/globe/ideas/articles/2007/08/04/the_downside_of_diversity**.

15 **"In nature, a diverse landscape"** … From an email to author from Deb Finck, director of Building Ohana, 2019.

16 **"Intimacy with difference"** ... Andrew Solomon, *Far from the Tree* (New York: Scribner, 2012), 6.

17 **"constituents have no energizer"** ... James Kruses & Barry Posner, *The Leadership Challenge: How to Keep Getting Extraordinary Things Done in Organizations* (San Francisco: Jossey-Bass, 1995), 79-80.

18 ***relational leading*** ... Lone Hersted and Kenneth J. Gergen, *Relational Leading: Practices for Dialogically Based Collaboration* (Chagrin Falls, Ohio: Taos Institute Publications, 2013), 27-31.

19 **following the work** ... Laurel Richardson, *Fields of Play: Constructing an Academic Life* (New Brunswick, New Jersey: Rutgers University Press, 1997), 185.

20 **"setting in motion"** ... Lone Hersted and Kenneth J. Gergen, *Relational Leading: Practices for Dialogically Based Collaboration* (Chagrin Falls, Ohio: Taos Institute Publications, 2013), 30-31.

21 **"ordinary courage"** ... Excerpt from conversation with local community leader, Sharen Allen, Champaign Illinois, 2019.

22 **"From a professional staff"** ... David Hopping, "*Community as Intervention: Modeling a Complex Intergenerational Neighborhood Initiative,*" Presented to the National Child Welfare Evaluation Summit, Washington DC, August 31, 2011.

23 **"...good managers provide"** ... Tom DeMarco & Timothy Lister, *Peopleware: Productive Projects and Teams* (New York: Dorset House Publishing Company, 1987), 141.

Chapter Thirteen

1 **"There is no use trying"** ... Lewis Carroll, *Through the Looking Glass,* (New York: Macmillan, *December* 1871), Chapter 5.

2 **David Brooks recently described** ... David Brooks, "A Generation Emerging from the Wreckage," *The New York Times,* September 26, 2018, A19.

3 **"Now I feel I have"** ... "*Bastion Community Reintegration Case Study,*" March 6, 2018. **https://www.joinbastion.org**.

4 **Ted Koppel quipped** ... Ted Koppel, "Hope for the Children," *Nightline,* aired October 3, 1996, American Broadcasting Company.

5 **"The weakest safety net"** ... Mark R. Rank, "The Cost of Keeping Children Poor," *The New York Times,* April 15, 2018.

6 **"...or to change the"** ... Dr. William Thomas, *What are Old People For? How Elders will Save the World* (Acton, MA: VanderWyk & Burnham, 2004), 179.

7 **"Loneliness and weak social connections"** ... Vivek Murthy, "Work and the Loneliness Epidemic," *Harvard Business Review, September 2017.* **https://**

hbr.org/cover-story/2017/09/work-and-the-loneliness-epidemic.

8 **Loneliness is so disabling** … Marvin Seligman, *Flourish* (New York: Free Press, 2011), 21.

9 **And the highly insightful** … Kenneth J. Gergen, *Relational Being: Beyond Self and Community* (New York: Oxford University Press, 2009).

10 **Recently, I came across** … Heerad Sabeti, "The Fourth Sector is a Chance to Build a New Economic Model for the Benefit of All," *Thrive Global*, September 17, 2017. **https://www.thriveglobal.com/stories/13959-the-fourth-sector-is-a-chance-to-build-a-new-economic-model-for-the-benefit-of-all**. All following quotes and references to Sabeti are from this source.

11 **the "citizen sector"** … also, referred to as "citizen base" by Ashoka, a global organization which envisions "a world in which everyone is a changemaker: a world where all citizens are powerful and contribute to change in positive ways." **https://www.ashoka.org/en-us/search?search_term=citizen+sector**.

12 **"Because it is fun."** … Marcus, writing as part of a commemorative tenth anniversary celebration of Hope Meadows in our national newsletter, *The Hope Herald*, Summer, 2004.

13 **"Darcel asked me,"** … Interview with David Hopping and Judith Pintar, November 14, 1007.

14 **"Usually when she comes"** … Residents participating in a focus group of Hope seniors, March 10, 2001.

15 **"I was tutoring Leon"** ... Ibid.

16 ***60 Minutes* correspondent** … Informal conversation between author and Lesley Stahl, April 2016.

17 **It was based on** … Kenneth J. Gergen, *Relational Being: Beyond Self and Community* (New York: Oxford University Press, 2009), 204.

18 **We have forgotten** … Christopher Alexander, *The Timeless Way of Building* (New York: Oxford University Press, 1979), 548-549.

Chapter Fourteen

1 **Neighborhood: "a term"** … George Galster. "On the Nature of Neighborhoods," *Urban Studies* 38 (12), 2001, 2011. **https://doi.org/10.1080/00420980120087072**

2 **Personal recovery has** … Dr. Larry Davidson, "Mental-Health Researchers Ask: What Is 'Recovery'?" *The New York Times,* February 25, 2020, D3.

3 **"From that moment"** … Author conversation with Deb Finck, August, 2019.

4 **But according to The ARC** … "Position Statements: Family Support,"

2020. This document can be downloaded at **https://thearc.org/wp-content/uploads/2019/08/16-117-The-Arcs-Position-Statements_C7_Family-Support-1.pdf**

5 **Nationwide, 2.6 million grandparents** …taken from "Grandfacts: National Factsheet for Grandparents and Other Relatives Raising Children," AARP, 2019. This document can be downloaded at **https://www.aarp.org/content/dam/aarp/relationships/friends-family/grandfacts/grandfacts-national.pdf**.

6 **So too, could Genesis** … Genesis is a Generations of Hope inspired intergenerational community of intentional neighboring. The information and quoted material in this paragraph can be found at **https://genesisdc.org**.

7 **"ageism," a term first** … Robert N. Butler, MD, *The Gerontologist*, Volume 9, Issue 4_Part_1, Winter 1969, 243-249.

8 **"negative stereotypes"** … Rylee A. Dionigi, "Stereotypes of Aging: Their Effects on the Health of Older Adults,"*Journal of Geriatrics*, August 2015.

9 **"To be caring of one" …** Barbara Tarlow, "Caring: A Negotiated Process That Varies," in S. Gordon, P. Benner and N. Noddings (Eds.), *Caregiving: Readings in Knowledge, Practice, Ethics, and Politics* (Philadelphia, Pennsylvania, University of Pennsylvania Press, 1996), 81.

10 **"Hope Meadows has elements"** … David Racine in an email exchange with David Hopping and author, July 23, 2010.

11 **"'I think this [project]'"** … Jeff Parrott, "South Bend Housing Project Would Pair Seniors With Young Adults Coming Out of Foster Care," *South Bend Tribune*. February 26, 2020. **https://www.southbendtribune.com/news/local/south-bend-housing-project-would-pair-seniors-with-young-adults-coming-out-of-foster-care/article_8a0350e8-5822-11ea-bc86-b7e39d3b8521.html#comments.**

12 **According to recent industry** … Data taken from Meyers Research & Zonda and Metrostudy, *Master Plan Community Report: 2019.* **https://meyersresearchllc.com/new-data-product-from-zonda-metrostudy-pinpoints-what-is-next-in-master-planned-communities/**.

13 Jonathan Davis, designer … Jonathan is the founder and principal architect of Davis Studio Architecture and Design, LLC in Bainbridge,Washington. He has applied his award-winning and community-minded micro-hood design to the development of Grow Community on Bainbridge, and worked closely with several emerging intentional neighborhoods to create accessible and connected neighborhood site and housing designs. You can visit his website at **https://davisstudioad.com.**

14 **Ross Chapin, the author** … Ross Chapin, *Pocket Neighborhoods: Creating Small-Scale Community in a Large-Scale World (Newtown, Connecticut, Taunton Press, 2011)*, 16.

15 **Katie McCamant and Charles Durrett** … read about their work to bring cohousing to North America at **http://www.cohousingco.com**.

16 **In Portland, Oregon** … Our Home at Cathedral Park. Visit the site at **https://www.ourhomeicc.org/interested-neighbors/our-home-cathedral-park/**.

17 **and near Charlottesville** … Visit this site at **https://www.hopefamilyvillage.org**.

18 **New Life Village** … Visit this site at **https://newlifevillage.org**.

19 **"the regeneration of"** … Dr. William Thomas, *What are Old People For? How Elders will Save the World* (Acton, MA: VanderWyk &Burnham, 2004), 280.

About the Author

photo credit: Cindy Krause

Brenda Krause Eheart, PhD is a leading authority on Intentional Neighboring. It was her research while at the University of Illinois that led to the realization of this concept through the creation of the first intentional neighborhood of its kind, Hope Meadows. She went on to found Generations of Hope, a nonprofit dedicated to the expansion of communities incorporating the intentional neighboring paradigm.

Brenda has received numerous honors, including *The Heinz Award in Human Condition*, the *AARP Inspire Award*, and recognition as a *Champion of Change* by the Obama administration. She also was named an *Ashoka Fellow* and a Civic Ventures *Purpose Prize Fellow*. Her work has been honored by three presidential administrations, including as a featured speaker at the closing of the inaugural Obama Foundation Summit for the Obama Presidential Library.

Hope Meadows has been featured in prominent broadcast and print media including, *ABC Nightline*, CBS's *60 Minutes*, *The Oprah Winfrey Show*, *The New York Times*, and NPR's *All Things Considered*. Retired from her position as executive director of Generations of Hope, Brenda continues to provide clear values and a cohesive vision for the intentional neighboring movement exploding in this country. She lives in Champaign, Illinois with her husband, J. Wayland Eheart, and their dog Chloe.

Made in the USA
Columbia, SC
25 October 2021

47829805R00162